THIS BOOK WILL GET YOU HIRED!

THIS BOOK WILL GET YOU HIRED!

Francois Philippe Fontaine

Table of Contents

Chapter 1
Does This Happen to You?

Your bills are mounting up. Your salary barely covers your expenses or – worse – you're one of the unfortunate ones without a job! You're dipping into your savings – even edging into debt. You're waking up every morning with a knot in your stomach, reluctant to tell your loved ones just how precarious things have become. A new position appears in your feed. Hurray! You decide to apply. It's not your dream job, but the pay's attractive, and surely anything's better than this gnawing fear.

Application

You make sure you do everything right. You sculpt your resume like Michelangelo creating a work of art. Perhaps you even hire a professional to do it for you. You've read your cover letter a million times over to correct the tiniest errors. Everything's perfect! You send it off and wait excitedly. Your wait turns out to be days, which turn into weeks and then into months. No response from them! You follow up by phone and e-mail. Still, no reply! At best, you get a canned response like "That person's not here right now" or "We're looking into it." This happens over and over again till you lose hope that you will ever escape this exhausting grind.

Interviews

Finally, your resume got shortlisted! You're called in for an interview. You put on your best suit, wear your brightest smile and walk in with your head held high. The questions they ask are boilerplate, such as "Tell me about yourself" and "Why are you leaving your current job?" You answer them the best you can, hoping that the interviewer's convinced. The truth is you're under so much pressure that you can't tell if you're winning or losing. You cross your fingers and hope for the best.

Round after round of interviews means, surely, you must be on the right track... right? In one session, you have a great conversation with the interviewer. They seem so nice. You leave feeling elated. Perhaps, this is the one. They said they'll get back to you soon and you dare to believe it's true.

Again, days turn into weeks and weeks into months. It's happening again! With almost every interview, you've heard nothing back. Now your morale is lost.

You seem to wonder what you did wrong. You beat yourself up: "How can I not be good enough, after putting in all this effort?" You replay your words and actions; blame yourself for every tiny mistake. You do nothing but wonder what made you miss the mark.

"Why Didn't I Get the Job?"

If all your experience and qualifications align perfectly with the role, why didn't you get the callback? This is a common problem. This would probably be the #1 pet peeve of every job seeker.

Oftentimes, the problem is not you. There are various factors at play in the background that most job seekers find hard to fathom.

For starters, recruiters are under mammoth pressure from top management and company policy. Expectations and bureaucracy often make them inefficient. That HR team that rejected your application last week probably knows you are well qualified! However, their bosses have a narrow vision of what they want. If your application deviates from that narrow vision by so much as half an inch, hirers are under massive pressure to reject you or else face a grilling from their superiors.

I want you to imagine your friend is interviewing for the same position as you. You know for a fact that he/she is terrible at this type of job. They have scant experience and hardly any chance of winning. You both leave the building at the same time. Turns out, they walk out clutching a job offer! Bam, you just entered the Twilight Zone!

Sadly, this sort of thing happens all the time. Recruiters can be terrible judges of both character and aptitude. The fact is, beyond taking a resume on faith, most organizations lack any means of measuring how qualified a candidate really is. As a result – I hate to say it, but – those willing to exaggerate their credentials often do better.

So How Do We Win?

It is unfortunate that we are in this situation right now, and as job seekers, we have no control over it. The best thing to do is to try and work around this mess. We need to stay in this messy system and still get what we want.

In every recruitment scenario, there are countless factors at play, under the surface, which is difficult to understand at first glance. The real key to winning is to understand every facet of the hiring process *from the employer's perspective*.

Up till now, your mind is probably fully prepared for the role of an employee, but once you read this book, all that changes. From now on, as you prepare for interviews, you'll be thinking from the point of view of an HR recruiter of your target company.

Your superpower is empathy.

Ask yourself, what would you have done if you were in charge of recruiting? Just like us, recruiters are human beings too. Every recruiter and every company is different. What they're seeking is sometimes not consistent, sometimes not even logical: it doesn't matter. Our job is to deeply understand the person and the situation we're dealing with. We'll look past what they *say* they want and discover what they are really looking for.

Remember we talked about a company's narrow vision? Going forward, we're going to show off your best qualities *only within that narrow vision* of what the company truly seeks. We'll prepare custom answers to all the common interview questions, keeping that company ideal firmly in mind.

And by the time you're done with this book, you'll no longer have to ask yourself, "Why didn't I get the call?" You'll understand – and you'll have a new method of preparation that puts you miles ahead of the competition.

Let's begin.

<u>Chapter 2</u>
The Typical Mindset of an Interviewer/Recruiter

When we apply for a job, we always like to think that the recruiters give our application its fair attention. We imagine them scanning our whole resume from top to bottom, reading every word exactly how it's intended. We might even hope that they value our humble achievements and overlook the flaws.

All this is possible in a unicorn-filled, rainbows-and-sunshine kind of world. In reality, your application is only as good as the mood of the hirer that day! On a day they feel good, they may give your application its due consideration. This is the best-case scenario. Even so, if they found the right candidate before they got to your application, the rest of the pile, including yours, goes to trash.

Sounds harsh now, doesn't it? But, there's more. Many companies have assigned this application filtering work to software bots called Applicant Tracking System. In theory, this system is supposed to look for keywords that relate to the job requirements. That's the party line, anyways. In reality, these systems are programmed to reject as many applications as possible without any human interference. There's no check in place to see whether these bots are in fact rejecting the truly unfit candidates or selecting only the right ones. So, chances are a cyber bouncer has randomly denied you entry before a live pair of eyes got involved.

Once you get past the application stage, sitting through interviews is a whole different ball game. You might think a well-qualified and experienced interviewer would have prepared the right set of questions to ask you. You're confident they'll aptly assess your fit for the role. In a world where pineapple is a type of apple, sure, this is true. In reality, though, this is a luxury that only few candidates get to enjoy. When it happens, it's a great experience to attend a well-put-together interview. On the flipside, the unprepared interviewers are greater in number than you think. This is why you feel they ask unnecessary or irrelevant questions sometimes.

I understand this is too much of a harsh reality to absorb in the first few paragraphs. Nonetheless, understanding the interviewer's mindset is your first and most important weapon against this unfair battle. It prepares you mentally and gives you a massive winning advantage.

<u>Recruiters Are Always in a Hurry to Fill Positions</u>

Have you noticed that almost every job opening these days is "urgent"? It's like hiring managers are always in a bomb-defusing mode. No joke, HRs and hiring managers are genuinely under pressure to fill positions as quickly as possible.

They have little to no time to go through applications. Even when they do, they only get to go through the most visible, surface-level details. Any application that's badly formatted, illegible or longer than one page (low-level positions) is already on a one-way trip to the trash can.

Imagine you open YouTube on your phone and go through the recommended videos. Chances are you'll probably only click on the best-looking, best-formatted thumbnail. This is true regardless of whether the actual video is good enough or not. It's difficult to judge how good a YouTube video is going to be based purely on the title or thumbnail, but there's no other way.

It's a similar situation for the recruiters. They are flooded with hundreds, or even thousands, of applications every day. They can't possibly go through all those applications. So, they give only a few seconds' glance to every application before deciding whether to select or reject it. On an average, it's estimated that a recruiter spends a mere 6-7 seconds on every application! If this number is anything to go by, you should make the best attributes of your resume noticeable within those 6-7 seconds. Make those precious seconds count.

During the interview stage, employers are hard-pressed for time all the more. They want to get more interviews done under less time. Mental fatigue often sets in when they have to sit through hundreds of people answering the same questions (often giving the same answers) over and over. It gets too repetitive too soon. Half the time, interviewers have difficulty actively listening to a candidate's answers. If you're so unfortunate to be among the last set of interviewees (which you typically won't know), they may not engage well with you. However, they will appreciate it if you were understanding of such things and showed empathy in this situation. They'll appreciate it more if you can give different, more thoughtful answers to the interview questions than the rest of the candidates. This will be a nice change of pace for them.

On top of all this, hirers also have to deal with the disappointment of not finding the right hire despite interviewing numerous candidates. They dread the fact that they have to face grilling from their bosses for not filling the position within time. Worse, even if they found the right candidate, there's a chance that the candidate turns down this job offer. This is when some employers force those candidates into accepting the job offer. Any employer who forces you into accepting a job you don't want is never a good employer. You should never work for an employer like that unless you want to do some serious facepalming in the future.

Recruiters Are Rewarded if They Fill a Position Quickly and at a Low Salary

While the job description might say that they want only the absolute best candidate, they may not actually want them! The job description is just a wish list. It's like a kid drawing a unicorn on paper and asking mommy to buy one exactly like it. Many recruiters already know this too.

Forget the best candidate – most recruiters don't want any candidate who is beyond "just good enough". They know that a highly competent candidate will also negotiate for a higher salary. Thus, recruiters are okay with a candidate who just meets the minimum aptitude level but agrees for a lower salary. Most of their effort actually goes toward making doubly sure that the candidate won't be trouble for them later on. Not only in terms of salary negotiation but also in terms of people skills, cooperation and expecting higher positions down the line. So, during the interview rounds, interviewers test the attitude and behavior of the candidate. Any red flag here means permanent rejection. Very few candidates are given the benefit of doubt.

While hiring the most qualified candidate is the official slogan, what they are really hiring is the least risky candidate within the skills and salary range. Once they have found that least risky candidate, they'll pressure that candidate into accepting a lower salary using numerous tactics. In essence, if you want to get a higher salary, it really depends on how desperate they are for a candidate, how many passable candidates there are besides you, how tough they want to negotiate and the usual market salary range for that position.

Yours Is Not the Only Position They Hire for

This one must be obvious. Still, many people make the mistake of thinking HR personnel or hiring managers are concerned about only one position. They often interview many candidates and for several different positions all at the same time. It's easy for them to get things mixed up.

For instance, they may mistake you for someone else just because you resemble them or your name sounds similar. Then, they'll apply all the positive or negative qualities of that other candidate on you! Extremely unfair, but happens all the same!

Other times, HR recruiters may pretend to have confused you for someone else just to force you into leaving or taking up another position you didn't apply for. If this happens, run! You have a major red flag here for a terrible employer. You certainly don't want to work for this organization even if your only other option is being trapped in a room with a telemarketer for eternity!

Most Recruiters Have No Idea What the Position Really Involves

This may sound counterintuitive especially if you have less experience attending interviews. Job positions come in all shapes and sizes these days. It's impossible for a recruiter to remember or understand what each position involves. Even some managers have no idea what their direct subordinates do. Thus, mixing up positions happens time and again.

For instance, it's common for HRs or hiring managers to confuse personal assistant with executive assistant, project manager with product manager, data analyst with business analyst, designer with developer, or copywriter with copyeditor. Also, misunderstanding the technical requirements of a role is commonplace. I've seen hirers assume Java and JavaScript to be the same thing as well as GFX and VFX, financial accounting and cost accounting, server admin and network admin, and so on. So, a Java expert might be asked to take up a JavaScript job, or a GFX professional a VFX job. Many recruiters fail to see the difference even when pointed out.

The opposite of this is not understanding that the same position or skill can have two different names. Customer Service Executive vs. Client Support Associate, Human Resources vs. Personnel Department, HTML vs. frontend web development, SQL vs. database are but a few examples. Say, you mentioned during the interview that you're an expert in SQL and you have handled almost every type of work there is in SQL. The technically illiterate manager or HR might still reject you because the job description only mentions the word "database" and you didn't mention database in your application or interview.

I can totally understand that not getting the job because of these silly misunderstandings can be quite frustrating. It is something outside your control and unfairly so.

If some hiring managers and HRs are ignorant of what the role really involves, it goes without saying that they also have no clue on how to assess your technical capability. When you explain how good you are with technical words, they only pretend to understand. This definitely gives an unfair advantage to those candidates who use nontechnical words and mention the expected keywords in the right places.

Having said all this, I don't mean to paint every recruiter with the same brush. There are very knowledgeable and prudent recruiters also. I have seen only a handful of such people, but they did impress me when I met them. They were a breeze to interview with and highly proficient at assessing one's skill level. They also empathized with how difficult some of the job responsibilities can be and how clients expect employees to perform unrealistic miracles. It's not usual to meet one of these people but you'd be really lucky if you did.

Sometimes They Ask Questions Just for the Heck of It

If you've doubted this already, here is your confirmation. Most people like to think the interviewer already has a lot of experience interviewing candidates. This could be true with some of them. However, there is also a whole group of interviewers who are totally new to the role. They may be as good at conducting an interview as a fish is at riding a bicycle. To cover up their lack of experience, they tend to ask unrelated questions.

Many recruiters often take inspiration from big companies. Sometimes, the top management pushes them to take that inspiration. One way or the other, they end up asking tough and complicated questions for entry-level roles. They think this makes them seem bigger, more knowledgeable and professional in the eyes of the candidate. It's understandable that everybody wants to show themselves to be better than they really are. However, doing this for smaller roles has the opposite effect. Unnecessarily tough questions have the potential to creep out good candidates and shoo them away faster than you can say "hired".

In a different light though, some questions are asked just to get you talking just to see how you communicate. This also buys the interviewer some time to think of the next question.

Stress Interview (aka Insulting Interview)
I have no intention of scaring you, but these type interviews do happen. They call you in as usual, but the moment you get in, they'll keep finding fault with

everything you say or do. They'll hurl any insult they can get at you. The point is to drive you to the limits of your patience to see how you react. They do this under the pretext of "testing" the candidate for his/her stress or anxiety threshold.

It's totally possible that the job involves a lot of stress and they want to make sure you can handle it. However, this may not be the only or even the most likely reason. Most companies will never attempt to show how stressful their workplace really is during the interview stage. Every company wants to appear as a great place to work. The actual reasons they conduct stress interviews could be much more nefarious.

Chances are they have already selected the candidate they want, usually internally or through recommendation. Maybe the CEO's son wants that job but doesn't want anybody to know. The interview is just a sham to show they're giving everybody a fair chance and are hiring only the "right" candidate. In some companies, they need to show the top management that they've tried hard to hire from the open market but couldn't find the right candidate. This might be to justify an internal hiring. If you're one such unfortunate applicant attending this sham, I truly feel for you. I've attended a number of stress interviews myself. To such interviewers, you're just another number for the record who needs to be disposed of as quickly as possible. Insult is the best tool they got.

The above is actually a better scenario. The worse is there are some interviewers who derive sadistic pleasure from triggering you. They just advertise non-existent jobs called ghost jobs (company requirements), but call you in for the interview just to take out their frustrations on you. It may take a while, probably a few seemingly normal rounds, before you can guess you've been invited to an insult interview. It could come as a rude shock when you realize it. Your confidence and self-esteem might take a massive blow from these experiences. I know this feels worst, but this is the sad reality for many applicants out there.

You have no idea of knowing for sure beforehand, and in many cases, you can't report or sue them. The best preparation you can do is to check in advance if there are any online reviews that mention this. Reviews are by no means foolproof but it is the best option one might have. Supposing you got caught in one of these interviews, I suggest you best get out.

Even if you're someone who takes it all in good sport, you have to realize that your everyday job in this company could be much worse. Remember, the interview is just a sample of the company culture. Even if you feel you have a high threshold for stress and you can survive this job, you still probably don't want to spoil your health by working such a job. The best thing to do is leave. While you're at it, leave a review somewhere online so that future applicants can easily notice it and be aware.

They Have to Like You

If you have successfully sidestepped all of the pitfalls above, there is still one more hurdle. Despite having well-defined job requirements and rigorous ways of testing every candidate, they only end up hiring whom they personally like. When it comes to this, they don't place any importance on the capability, qualifications, experience or even whether you were on your best behavior. They simply need to like you personally.

This is why they often end up hiring incompetent simpletons who don't even know the ABCs of that line of work. If you feel this is unfair, you're not alone. I am with you.

What makes one person like another is extremely subjective and personal. It often has no logical basis. It's spontaneous and emotional. The "liking" feeling is also temporary because you can't like someone all the time. There are times when you hate them too.

Having said this, there is a reason they do this. They want to make sure you fit into the company culture seamlessly. If the interviewer likes you, then chances are others in the company will too. This is usually what they mean by "being a good fit for the company".

This is not completely in your control. However, there are some factors you can control. They usually judge you by your looks, your dressing sense, hairstyle, how you talk, what you say, whether you frequently disagree, how you act or react, your thought process in answering questions, how you treat people and even whether you smile. There are probably many more points, but you get the idea here, don't you? Taking care of such simple things will massively increase your chances of being offered the job.

This essentially means that people skills always outweigh technical skills. A person with barely acceptable technical skills but excellent people skills will immediately get hired over the vice versa.

Chapter 3
Optimize Your Approach

Most applicants prepare for an interview thinking "Will I get this job?" As they get dressed for the interview, "Will they select me?" repeatedly comes to mind. "What salary will I get?" flashes in their head as they travel to the interview place. Once they enter the place, "Is this where I'll work once selected?" they wonder.

While this self-focus is nothing wrong, and is quite natural given the situation, it may be working against you! Let me explain. When you begin your thoughts with you in the center, consciously or subconsciously, you start acting selfish. This is a natural psychological occurrence for everybody. "So, what's wrong with being selfish?" you ask?

Recruiters absolutely hate self-centered candidates. They conduct job interviews precisely for this reason. They want to find out whether you think only about yourself or you have also given enough thought about *them* before applying. Of course, they also check a million other things, but the bottom line is a selfish employee could be detrimental to the company.

If you can completely avoid being selfish, great – nothing like it. But, for most people, it's very difficult. So, the practical thing to do is to never show your selfishness. Choose every word you speak and every action you do carefully such that you don't expose any selfishness.

 Now, how to not show selfishness when you want the job just to pay your bills in the first place? I know, it's very difficult, but required if you want to win.

Here is where empathy comes in. In this context, empathy doesn't mean feeling sorry for the recruiters. It means to actually think about this whole process from their viewpoint. Think beforehand what the recruiter or manager hopes to achieve by filling this position. What's going on inside their heads right now? What do they like to see in you? How relieved would they feel if they can fill this position today with the right candidate? How happy would they be if you turned out to be the perfect candidate they've been searching all along? If you have ever worked in recruitment or been a hiring manager, imagining this could be much easier for you.

Understanding the Expectations

Using their own job description, picture in your mind all the qualities they want to see in the ideal candidate. Do note that, for the same job, each employer might have different expectations. For instance, you might think being perfect in your daily work makes you the ideal candidate. Maybe that particular employer isn't looking for perfection. In their mind, an ideal candidate could be one who is regular to work and comes on time! Carefully studying what they want is crucial. Good thing is most job ads will usually mention their expectations, directly or indirectly.

Do some imagining about all this before deciding to apply. You want to take ample time at this stage. Having a more concrete mental picture of what's expected will help you send a successful application and answer most of the interview questions correctly. Doing this exercise will also help you choose the right job for yourself and avoid jobs you don't really want.

If you have no clue what the hirer wants, at least make an educated guess. This could prove mighty useful later on as you'll have some basis to work with.

Submitting Your Application

This is the stage where recruiters shortlist a handful of candidates out of a swarm of applications. What'll you do if you were the recruiter going through thousands of applications and having to pick the best from it? You might think it's like finding a needle in a haystack. But no, that'd be far too easy. This one is more like finding the best needle from a needle stack!

Imagine you read application after application all day long and you never find the right hire. You look at the clock and it's time to go home, but your desk is still full of applications! How exhausting!! In this situation, wouldn't you be happy if your burden was reduced? Wouldn't it let off some steam if you pick the most pleasing-looking, prominent applications? While you're at it, why not also pick the "safest" applications – the ones that your boss is least likely to question later on?

Now, switch back to being an applicant and apply this understanding. If you want to get shortlisted, make your resume easy to pick. It's as simple as that.

Make every line in your resume short, clear and pleasing to read.

Start your resume with the current or most recent job experience that's relevant to the job you apply for. Experience in the same or a similar job role is what employers value most. If you have been in the job market for more than a handful of years, experience is all the more important. For recent graduates or those with scanty work experience, educational qualifications play a major role.

With the magic of formatting, make sure the most relevant attributes are in bigger, bolder writing while the less relevant traits are either removed or are barely visible. Likewise, make your resume more readable by using subheads and bullet points wherever possible. Most recruiters read only headings and bullets while ignoring paragraphs.

Most of all, keep your resume within a single page. This is extremely important. Unless your work experience spans several decades and the position you're applying for is right at the top, you should keep your resume within a single page. Besides being easy to read, one-page resumes are also easy to carry around in printed form and store for later reference.

When writing the resume, definitely mimic the same keywords used in the job ad. The wording used in the job ad is most likely what everyone uses within the organization. Using a different term might make them think you're not qualified. On the other hand, using the same term will subconsciously tell them that you think like them, which in turn will make you look like a good fit for the company.

Much of what I've said for the resume is also true for the cover letter. Many employment consultants (or anybody who gives advice on job applications) often ignore the cover letter. Matter of fact, there are some who even advise against including a cover letter. It's tempting to argue that writing tailor-made cover letters for every application takes too much time. Yep, it does take time. Also, the second argument is that many recruiters don't have time to read cover letters, and so, it's a waste of time to write them anyways. Yep, some recruiters don't have time. However, cover letters do get read more than you think!

Imagine that situation where a recruiter does take time to read your letter. You want to make the best use of this situation. To the recruiter, a cover letter makes your application a more human-to-human interaction than a "read-resume-select", "read-resume-reject" routine. In other words, you want your cover letter to be that diamond in the rough that stops their mindless doomscrolling and grabs their conscious attention.

It's your chance to talk directly to the recruiter who might very well be the hiring manager – the one who could be your potential boss. Through the letter, you can clearly tell them, within reason, all the ways in which you match their expectations. It's one way for the recruiter to understand who you are and how you communicate. A sincere cover letter is a great way to make a positive impression even before a recruiter or interviewer sees your face or hears your voice.

It's estimated that even in the easiest-to-get jobs, the recruiters usually reject an average of 75% of the applications. That means a job with a hiring rate of 25% is the easiest you can get! For the most competitive jobs, we are looking at a rejection rate of 99% or more. Your chance of succeeding is less than 1%! Let that sink in for a moment. In this situation, one of the accessible ways by which you can stand out is writing a short but aptly worded cover letter.

All in all, you want your application to be short, clear and easily noticeable. In the resume stage, you have little control over the process. To increase your chances, you want to be as humble and polite as possible both in your resume and cover letter. I've seen candidates get selected only because their wording was polite and they said exactly what the recruiter wanted to hear.

Written Test

In some companies, you might be required to sit for a written test. The test could be anything from a technical aptitude test, communication skill test or professional writing capability test to a personality/psychology test, current affairs test, stress test or something else.

Depending on each company's selection process, they may give this test at any stage they want or skip it for you altogether. The passing criteria for such a test could be anything the examiner decides.

Of course, it pays to know what type of test it is and prepare for it beforehand. Mostly, this'll be informed in advance especially if it needs preparation. In case they only told you "There'd be a written test" but didn't tell you what type of test it's going to be, it's always okay to call up and ask.

Don't hesitate to directly ask them how to prepare for this test. This will put a positive impression on you because you show that you care about preparing for the test. Also, try to gather what it is that they expect out of this test. Ask them the minimum passing score, what makes a good score and what is excellent. If the person who speaks with you is open to it, also ask them the method they'll use to judge the result.

Then again, they may not be open to revealing anything also. They may want to take you by surprise. In such a case, they'll either inform you about the test only at the last minute or may misinform you about the type of test. If either happens, don't take it personally. Don't get nervous. Politely ask for a reschedule so that you get time to prepare. If they agree for a reschedule, you can use the meantime to prepare. If they give you no opportunity to prepare, it's still okay. Go in boldly and do your best. That's probably what they want to see – how well you perform without preparation.

In either case, remember that not all tests require you to score the maximum. Sometimes, the minimum passing score might be sufficient. Other times, they may be very happy to find someone familiar with the subject at all, let alone answer it well. For all you know, you could be a sight to sore eyes.

First Round of Interview

Congratulations! They've shortlisted you. You're now called in for an interview. This means they are already fairly convinced of your technical capabilities and work experience – aka hard skills. Now, they want to evaluate your soft skills.

An interview can be described as a soft skills competition. It's a situation where every candidate competes to show their best side in terms of people skills, communication and attitude. In other words, you need to show that you're better than other candidates at how you deal with people, how you talk, what your thought process is like, what your interests are, how you see the company, how serious you are about this job and so on. Interviewers will note how agreeable you are, how your personality will match with others already working in the team and whether your personal values align with the company culture.

One of the best suggestions I can give here is to get the interviewer to imagine you in the role! Make sure every word you say creates a mental image of you in the role. For instance, instead of saying "This job requires multitasking", tell them "As the Product Manager, I'll smoothly handle several tasks at once including customer calls, team meetings, product research, cost accounting etc. without any problem". Ask questions, talk about your performance or elaborate your strengths in such a way that the interviewer needs to imagine you performing in the role.

This technique alone will dramatically increase your chances of getting hired. There is a simple psychological reason for this. Once we form a mental picture of some act, we tend to do it more readily. Thus, if you can plant in their mind the picture of you performing well in the role, you'll subconsciously create trust. Needless to say, this will easily get you hired.

Interviewing is a whole different ball game from submitting applications, mind you. There is no fixed formula for winning or even answering questions. It just depends on you, them and the situation.

Interview Anxiety

Does job interview give you the jitters? Do you tremble with a gut-wrenching panic that grips you by the throat and refuses to let go? Is there a fear of failure, rejection or even the vulnerability of being exposed to the harsh judgments of others?

Interview anxiety can be a very intense and exhausting feeling but is also surprisingly easy to conquer. While everybody worries about a job interview, you could be a great deal more nervous if you're less experienced. Much of the worry comes from the fear of the unknown. You don't know what kind of company you're about to step into, the people you're going to meet or the type of questions they might ask.

The only way to put aside such worries is to attend more and more interviews. The more you attend, the more you know. In fact, there's nothing wrong with attending a few interviews for jobs you don't even want, just to get some practice. This will magically boost your confidence by a great deal.

Before going in for an interview, always look up the organization's reviews online and specifically if they mention anything about interviews. Online forums and Q&A platforms can also be a great resource. Insulting interview experiences and sham jobs will usually be mentioned as such. Also, you can find specific interview questions asked by particular companies for particular roles. Very handy, eh?

While it's all good, be wary that you may find fake reviews and mixed reviews. Of course, it can be off-putting. The good news is at least some of the reviews will mention the truth. You just have to read between the lines. I know, it's easier said than done. For starters, find out if the majority of the reviews have mentioned the same thing. If many people have had the same experience, then you can be sure there will be some truth to it. You can evade troublesome interviews or jobs this way.

More than online reviews, if you can find a trustworthy friend or contact who has ever worked in that company, that would be most ideal. This may be difficult to do but totally worth it. When you do find someone like that, keep in mind that they may be reluctant to share some of the things, especially the negatives. They fear that they may come off as badmouthing their previous employer and this could seriously affect their future.

Thus, make sure the person you decide to ask will tell you at least the partial truth. If they want to tell you the truth but couldn't due to circumstances, they may indirectly hint at certain things. Make sure you pay close attention and read between the lines. If they mention any negative, you might want to amp it up a few notches to get the true picture.

These are some of the ways in which you can ease your pre-interview worry.

Truth be told, interviewers often worry more about the interview than the candidates themselves. The hirer has the harder job here. Even a single mishap or wrong hire could mean that their job is on the line. Thus, putting your interviewer to ease about these worries is half the battle won already. Let me explain.

Worries of an Interviewer

When interviewing a candidate, interviewers often tend to think of all the bad employees they've had in the past.

Let's see now... they first had that guy Absent Adam who was never on his seat – frequently going on long breaks and taking one too many leaves. Then, they had this dame Idle Ida – not at all productive, taking too long for basic tasks and always wanting to leave early. Then came

Savage Sam – was polite during interviews but later became an insubordinate, rude, bullying troublemaker. Oh, then Jane proved to be unqualified, they fired Bob for incompetence, Nathan had bad hygiene… well, you get the picture. They'd hate it if you turned out to be like one of these.

For every candidate who turns out to be a bad hire, recruiters and hiring managers face grilling from their bosses. Interviewing, training and bringing new employees up to speed cost companies a lot of money. If new employees come out not as expected, it's a huge unproductive expense for the company that can't be recovered. When more and more new employees turn out to be bad, these losses can easily add up. No joke, such losses could potentially bankrupt the company. So, recruiters want to make doubly sure they're hiring a safe bet.

As if all this isn't bad enough already, recruiters and hiring managers have even bigger worries too. Will you create more losses than the hiring and training expenses? That is to say, will you turn out to be like Jake who got the company into legal trouble? Or, are you another Sophie in disguise whose temper lost the company a good client? Will you follow in Mike's footsteps into leaking company secrets out? Or is Bill your inspiration for workplace harassment? Will you physically attack someone inside the office when provoked enough like big ol' Bruce did? Will you be careless enough to accidentally set something on fire (Oh, I still hate you for that, Emily)? Will you misplace important company files (thanks a lot, Sarah)? Will you steal company money (talking about you here, Jim)?

Such questions will keep popping in and out of their heads. These questions might seem too extreme to you, but these are the ways in which past employees have caused pain to them. Needless to say, interviewers want to avoid such things at any cost. They'd probably have a heart attack if any of this were to happen again. Obviously, they can't ask you these questions directly, and so, they find ways and means to indirectly assess your character, however right or wrong their methods may be.

Even if you're none of the above, and are hardworking and well behaved, you could still create a huge loss for the company if you decide to quit too soon. In recent times, the biggest concern of employers is attrition. It's no longer a question of whether an employee would leave but when. Hence, much of their questions will go toward finding out how much thought you've given about actually performing this role and how much you like it (or can bear it). Based on this, they'll indirectly make a judgment on how long you're likely to stay in this job.

What Does This First Round Mean to You?

Remember that an interview is a two-way street. It's not just a way for the employer to evaluate you but also one for you to evaluate the company and whether you want to work there. As such, your evaluation should begin the moment you enter the company premises. Right from the security guard and receptionist to the actual person you're supposed to meet, note how everybody treats you. What you really want to note is whether you're treated like a number or treated like an actual human being. This one alone says a lot about the company culture.

Are the people inside the company happy to see you or receive you? Does anyone attend to you within a reasonable amount of time? What's everybody's general temperament like – are they looking satisfied or frustrated? Are they professional in their speech and manner? While you wait, you might probably see bosses and subordinates walking around going about their business – how do they talk to each other, treat each other?

Did your interview begin on time? Did they make you wait a long time and was there a valid reason? During the interview, do they treat you like an equal or show their bossy side? Do they begin judging you straightaway or aim to create a positive impression about themselves first? Are their judgments well founded? Do they show ample sensitivity when asking difficult questions or is their tone in your face? Are they conducting the interview with full interest to get to know you or are they doing it as a chore? When discussing the terms of the job, do they push it down your throat or is their tone more matter of fact? At any point, do they show any concern for your preference or are they stubborn in their requirements?

The answers to the above questions are not just a simple yes or no. They can range across a wide spectrum. Much of all this is about how you feel. Trust your gut feeling. If you feel you won't fit in there, you won't. If at any point you feel this company will never work out for you, leave immediately.

Subsequent Rounds of Interviews

Companies have varying ideas on what makes up different rounds of interviews. There are some companies that consider interviewing with HR as the first round, immediate manager as the second round, next-level manager or maybe even the CEO (in case of some companies) as the final round of the interview. Some companies consider different rounds as simply various stages to eliminate candidates with hardly any difference in the rounds themselves. Others see the first round as an informal round with a single person and subsequent rounds as a more formal round with a higher-ranking manager or a panel. In case of a panel, they might have prepared tougher questions and different members of the panel might pry you for answers in quick succession (this could turn out to be a stress interview). In other companies, hirers may schedule ad hoc subsequent rounds that are similar to the first round meant to clarify more things with you. These different rounds can happen on different days or all on the same day.

Basically, it can be anything. It's very difficult to give a one-size-fits-all advice here. The best thing to do is to inquire about everything beforehand. Find out during your first phone call or during your first round of interview as to how many rounds they have planned. Always ask what every round is about and who'll interview you. Ask if it's going to be a one-on-one or a panel interview. It's also okay to ask how you should be prepared for each round. In most cases, they'll be happy you're putting in forethought. Asking this shows that you're actually interested in this job and want to make a good impression.

Mostly they'll tell you these things. Most companies in fact have a practice of informing these things in advance. In some rare but not unheard-of cases, they may suddenly plan a round. It may happen that they couldn't inform you before and inform you only on the spot. In such a case, you should still be prepared.

If the Interviewer Is HR

Human Resources personnel and hiring managers (who are going to be your bosses, if hired) are two major types of people who'll interview you. They may interview you separately or together. If they interview you separately, they'll exchange information about you later on. Strictly speaking, they are required to work together and decide on hiring you. However, in practice, HRs and managers may have different goals in mind.

An HR person would usually evaluate you from the company's perspective. They want you to fit into the organization's culture. HRs are the ones who oversee your application process from beginning to end. This includes background checks (past companies, educational institutions, past criminal records etc.), passing your application through various managers and teams, scheduling calls and interviews, serving as the link between you and the hiring manager, evaluating your expected salary etc.

HR questions and concerns are always about how hiring you will impact the company overall. When interviewing with an HR, always answer questions from the company's perspective. HRs will appreciate this.

If the Interviewer Is a Manager

A manager is usually only concerned about their team or division (group of teams). Every question they ask or every concern they have will usually be on the lines of how it'll affect their team. They want to see if you'll fit into the team's culture. The team's culture could be very different from company culture. Managers will evaluate how their team members will see you based on how you talk, think, and act. Even if there's nothing wrong with you, they may still reject you if they feel your behavior is different from their team's.

Another thing a manager is concerned about is subordination. They try to check if you will, once hired, talk back to them, disrespect them (or other team members) or show passive-aggressive resistance to their orders. Nobody wants to hire an insolent troublemaker. Of course, they'll also check if you'll turn out to be a slacker, expect to be spoon-fed, misunderstand instructions, be irresponsible, complain too much, gossip, act like a know-it-all, micromanage etc.

Fundamentally, the manager is the person who makes the final decision on you. Therefore, this is the person you want to focus more on. When the manager feels positive about you and has made a decision to hire you, the HR usually has no say on the matter.

When talking with the manager, show a lot of humility. Show that you're ready to listen to and understand everything they have to say. Demonstrate that you're interested in taking and fulfilling orders. This will go a long way.

Try to truly understand what the team is about, where it fits within the company, how your role in particular contributes to the team and so on. Summarize what the manager said to show that you've understood. Ask the right questions to show that you've given enough thought about actually performing this work. These simple things will make managers more willing to hire you over others.

If the Interviewer Is a Senior Member of the Team

Sometimes, a manager alone is not enough to find out whether you're technically qualified. A technical expert, who is usually a long-serving, veteran member of the team, will also be asked to do the interview. This person may speak with you one on one or may join along with the manager. If it's a panel interview, they may be part of the panel.

Their only goal during the meeting is to give an opinion on whether you're as good as you say you are at this job. In other words, they are there to break down your pretense of expertise, if you had put on one. The questions will usually be from an extremely practical standpoint that only a person with considerable experience can answer. This is a great way for them to eliminate those who lie about their experience and also those who don't apply their mind.

Their questions may range from soft testing to putting you on the spot. The number of times you say "I don't know" or answer in a way that indicates you don't know will be noted. The more questions you can't answer, the more they'll doubt your capability. They'll discuss their findings later on with the hiring manager later on.

While this might seem intimidating on the outset, this is a great opportunity to get to know who and what you're dealing with. From how they approach you and treat you, you can imagine how the team will function. From the type of questions they ask, you can guess the type of work you'll be doing every day on this job.

For the senior member of the team, show a lot of respect toward their expertise and seniority. In case you don't know the correct answer, make an attempt to figure out the most practical option for the given situation. Justify your answer with ample logic. Make sure your justification shows that you care about the company and the work you do. Whether or not you apply your mind to the context will be noted. The thing they hate the most is a textbook or robotic answer. They just need one impractical answer from you to reject your whole application. You want to get this right as much as possible. Having said this, some seniors may be more forgiving even if you don't know all the answers straightaway. However, they will note how much you try. They may be more interested in your approach than the actual answer.

Final Round

There are varying definitions of what a company might call "final round". From what the word suggests, this is the last step after which they'll decide whether to select or reject you. In some companies, this round mostly happens when they've decided to give you the job. It only involves handing over the job offer after some chitchat.

In other companies, final round is still another solid round of interview for them to eliminate more candidates.

There are those companies where the hirers can decide which round is in fact the final round. They can increase or decrease the number of rounds as and when they please!

Some hirers use the final round to clarify with you any detail they might have missed during the previous rounds. While this type of final round involves no elimination, you want to be careful not to mess up or create a bad impression.

In any type of "final round", always remember that this is still an interview. Even if they have already decided to hire you, talk to you informally and seem all nice, don't get too comfy. They may still change their mind at any time, based on anything you say or do. So, just answer the questions, keep smiling and keep your cool.

Bottom Line

An application process requires different approaches at each stage. While hard skills are important when sending the application, and will certainly get your foot in the door, it's good communication, people skills and humility that will ultimately get you hired. Always play your cards with the hirer's goals in mind. To make this happen, tailor your approach as per every situation. Remember, in the game of job hunt, winners are those who can bend without breaking.

Chapter 4
Impressions vs. Hard Reality

I had two friends in college – A and B.

A was the <u>Average guy who Advertises</u>. A was no specialist at anything but could do the bare minimum in every work. Beyond the surface level, he didn't care much about anything in life. I lost count on the number of times A was late to classes. He's the type of guy who'd score a perfect zero even in the easiest assignments and cheerfully smile about it. He'd turned up to exams (even finals) without studying a word! He made sure he got the minimum passing score but never bothered to actually learn anything.

Matter of fact, if he had any strength, then it was his people skills. He was super easygoing. Never took anything to heart. He knew how to charm almost everyone he met and took a genuine interest in others. I don't remember a soul that didn't fall for his sense of humor. Naturally, he was one of the most popular boys in college, had many friends and made an excellent reputation. He made sure he showed only his best side at all times. He knew how to paint a bright picture of almost anything and convince people to cooperate with him.

B, on the other hand, was the <u>Brainy but Boring</u> one of the class. Most people would call him a nerd. He was highly skilled at almost every activity, but never talked much. He had only a handful of superficial friends. He never wanted popularity or large social circles. He was more interested in becoming a technical expert in his field. You'd often find him reading specialized books of his subject. He was so well read that his questions often baffled professors. He could write his own textbook if they let him! He believed his knowledge and skills alone will land him a job.

Come graduation, everybody started hunting for a job. A and B had different strategies up their sleeves. A put together a resume that detailed all the small activities he did as a big deal. He mentioned every small thing from that one-hour seminar from years ago that everybody forgot about to a mandatory write-up on climate change we all had to submit. He listed the internships, private courses and some volunteering activities he took part in. There's no saying he did any of these activities sincerely, but he put them in all the same. He paid a professional resume designer to make sure everything was visually appealing. His resume sounded like he has had an all-round life with so much positivity. While this has nothing to do with the core skill sets required for the jobs he applied to, it made him sound like a highly motivated, confident and interesting individual to be around. This helped the recruiters visualize A as someone fun to work with, someone they'd love to have around in the office.

On the other hand, B was choosy about the jobs he applied to. He wanted a job in the same field as his study. He was very particular about the specialization. In his resume, he listed only those skills, qualifications and internship experiences that were pertinent. He listed nothing beyond what's required for the job, never overstated any of the activities or achievements. He used several technical terms and statistics to explain how productive he can be, hoping this will prove his competency. He formatted his resume plain and simple. No professional design or visually appealing elements, but everything he wrote was clear to read as plain text.

While attending interviews, A was always smiling, friendly and filled with energy. He was enthusiastically ready to explain anything the interviewers asked. His communication was great. His behavior was very professional, but at the same time, he also showed more of his social side. The interviewers felt good after interacting with him. The conversation went very well.

Then, it was B's turn. B was an introvert. The environment was nervously new to him. He had to put in considerable effort to hide his social anxiety and actually speak. He managed to answer all the technical questions correctly. The interviewers were convinced that he was as qualified as his resume said. They had no doubt about his technical aptitude. However, his too serious and to-the-point answers didn't make the interviewers feel any comfortable. They began uneasily moving in their seats. It was as if they suddenly got ants in their pants.

B used technical terms to explain what he can do for them. But all that went straight over their head. None of them were technical people and they couldn't follow him. It went as successful as explaining quantum physics to a room full of toddlers! His statistics on how efficiently he finished every piece of work only made them more uncomfortable. None of them had any mental energy left to process it. At a logical level, the interviewers quickly understood that B is the most capable candidate they had had in a while. However, they didn't feel very good after their interaction with him. It was his communication and social skills that left a bad aftertaste. After B left the interview room, there was an awkward silence for a long time.

No points for guessing who won. A not only had an easier time, but also got many job offers! He had the luxury that many didn't have – choice of job. He chose the best offer and went with it.

On the flipside, B had to repeatedly try. Since he was very specific about his specialization, he sent fewer applications. Also, his lack of social skills didn't help. He had to wait around for months before he received his first offer. His job search process on the whole was nothing short of backbreaking.

A and B from this story were polar opposites in many ways. Each was good at one thing and lacking in the other. We all would've seen several A's and B's in our lives and formed our own impressions. In fact, we have some amount of A and some amount of B inside of us. The percentages might differ though.

There are many lessons to be learned from this story. If I have to summarize the story of A and B in one word, I'd say "advertising". A knew how to effectively advertise himself or sell himself, while B didn't.

Advertising – Painting the Fanciful Picture

A job interview is much the same as a TV ad. The difference is that the product is you (as an employee) and you have to do it by yourself in person.

In the movie *North by Northwest*, Cary Grant's character says "In the world of advertising, there's no such thing as a lie. There's only expedient exaggeration." This is quite true for job interviews also. The one who lands the job is not the one most adept at doing the job but the best salesman. Of course, used car salesmen make excellent interview candidates!

When was the last time you got enamored by a TV ad? Chances are that the ad had some form of exaggeration going on. Say, you would've seen male deodorant ads where women blindly follow a man just because he wore that brand of deodorant. This is an exaggeration, quite improbable in real life.

Another great example is tortilla chips commercials. They often feature unbelievable situations such as grandmas becoming action heroes, unborn baby reacting to dad eating chips and what not! While being obviously illogical, these ads turned many heads.

Weight loss ads often show unrealistic "before" and "after" photos to overstate the amount of weight you can reduce. Skin care products almost always promise to make you 10 years younger. Cleaning products always promise to make your house squeaky clean without even scrubbing. Every toothpaste ad promises to make your teeth sparkling white. The list goes on.

What do all of these ads have in common? Is there any pattern you can notice here? For one, none of these ads aim to be logical. Everyone knows none of these promises are going to happen in real life. The outcomes shown are so extremely exaggerated that you're often left confused. What's more, some of these ads show outcomes nobody wants in real life. For instance, some car commercials show flying cars but nobody expects their car to fly in real life (at least not yet).

The only motive of these ads is to grab your attention, and grab your attention they did. Once they grab your attention, you remember the ad. Thanks to that, you remember the brand. You remember the brand, you ask for it at the store – Lo and behold, they make the sale. Do you see the point here?

Such ads may seem ridiculous at first, but they work! Ads that exaggerate the result make a stronger and more memorable impression that people want to try that product at once. While a flying car isn't real yet, car owners love to imagine as if they're flying. It's not the product itself but the idea that people fall in love with. Exaggeration is an age-old, time-tested formula that just works.

Intentionally or not, many candidates have applied this formula to their job search and found success. It's surprising how many interviewers buy into their exaggerated claims. While some interviewers may willingly believe such claims, many of them have no option but to decide based on these claims. As we saw before, managers need to justify their hiring decisions to their bosses. A candidate with attractive qualities in their profile (even if exaggerated) and a strong claim of high performance (even if exaggerated) is an easier justification compared to a candidate without these things. It's no longer a test of how capable a candidate truly is but a measure of how capable the candidate confidently *claims* to be.

Of course, there are always some sharp-witted hirers who won't buy into this. But, such hirers are rare! In the vast majority of cases, hirers give more attention to the exaggerating applicant.

Exaggeration vs. Lying

At this point, you may have several questions.

- Exaggeration is wrong, isn't it?
- Isn't it unethical to make false claims?
- Isn't exaggeration the same as lying on my resume?
- What if my employer finds out later on?
- Could I land into trouble?
- How do I answer any embarrassing questions when they find out?

These are fair questions. First up, exaggeration is not the same as lying.

A lie is something you can't justify, but exaggeration is something you can! In other words, you have to take some positive you already have and blow it up out of proportion (exactly like TV ads). Such exaggeration is necessary to grab the recruiter's attention. Explain your positives in several alluring words and phrases that would be music to the recruiter's ears. Portray yourself as the magic candidate they've been searching for years.

While you're at it, never lie in your resume. I am completely against lying. I've seen too many candidates suffer because they claimed to be good at things they can hardly do. Lying in your resume is the quickest way to lose credibility.

However, exaggeration has hardly been a problem. It only beautifies your already existing qualities and makes you a more appealing candidate in the eyes of the recruiter. What you're essentially doing is decorating your best side and presenting it with gloss. The attractiveness will make the hirer choose you over others.

If you still feel hesitant, remember that companies do make false claims themselves. They go to great lengths to prove that they have the best work environment and opportunities for growth, even if it may be untrue. They also have tall, unfulfillable expectations about the "ideal" candidate. Given these things, it's no wonder that applicants are stretching the truth like a bungee cord just to get their foot in the door.

Many hiring managers have gotten used to hiring exaggerating candidates and finding out later on that they're not as good. Many managers see exaggerating candidates more as an easy justification to their bosses than as a potential letdown. The pressure put on them to immediately justify their hiring decisions is far greater than the pressure to hire the right candidate. Thus, most of these claims, even when found out to be exaggeration later on, go unquestioned as long as the exaggerator fulfills the bare minimum and causes no trouble.

Big Name is Big Game

Employers value more a candidate from a highly reputable work organization or educational institution. If a resume mentions a well-known, esteemed organization, that candidate automatically soars in value regardless of their actual skills.

The general assumption is that a candidate from that organization would work at a higher standard. They're likely to have a lot of knowledge and experience. While this generalization might be true at a broader level, it may or may not apply to that candidate in particular. For all we know, that candidate could be the bottom-of-the-barrel, untalented slacker whom the organization wanted out the first chance they got. That candidate may be the one who worked or learned only the bare minimum without applying their mind.

However, hirers still value such a candidate over someone from a little-known organization with a great performance record. This is by no means fair. Then again, talking from the hirer's viewpoint, hiring such a candidate is easy to justify to their bosses.

Also, be wary that if you've studied or worked in a highly reputed organization yourself, it would be a huge value addition to your resume merely on the outset. It'll definitely help you get your foot in the door. You might even win any interview hands down. However, if you want to survive and grow in the job market, your skill set is what actually matters. Big names can definitely help you but only so much.

Smoke and Mirrors

If you feel this whole process is too fake to handle, it sure is. Getting a job and holding on to it is a make-believe game. Matter of fact, any type of career is going to need some amount of make-believe. Most people you meet in any job or business will often expect you to keep up such pretenses. Sure, it's very difficult to play this game. However, in the present job market, this is a very necessary game. Better get used to it.

Most companies and hiring personnel are so proficient at this. Often what they say they want and what they really want are different. For instance, a company that advertises for a confident interview candidate might actually hate it if a candidate is truly confident. A truly confident candidate will see through their pretense, ask the right questions, weed out lies and negotiate firmly for a higher salary. These are all qualities companies hate.

When they say "confident", what they really mean is confident enough to work on your own without assistance, but not at all confident enough to negotiate or question authority even when necessary. In other words, they want a yes-man who acts as if they are confident. Obviously, they can't say that in the ad so directly. So, they use specific words and phrases that need to be read between the lines. Every word an employer says in the job posting, in the interview and once you start work needs to be carefully scrutinized for the real meaning.

For instance, employers often use "self-learner" to mean no training will be given, "self-motivated" to mean this job will be demoralizing, "excellent opportunity" to mean no opportunity, "flexible" to mean boundaries will be violated and "team player" to mean abusive coworkers. You'll need to decode more such words by yourself.

Again, I am not trying to be negative or paint every employer with the same brush. Just sharing what happens out there.

Should You Apply for a Job Posting with High Expectations?

You would've definitely seen such job ads – a huge list of unrealistic expectations that very few people might meet. New graduates often complain that even entry-level jobs ask for several years of experience! You might wonder who might actually meet those expectations and apply for such a job.

This is another one of those mind games companies play with candidates. In today's job market, the candidate pool is ever increasing while the number of desirable jobs is dwindling. This means that companies are bombarded with hordes of applications, most of which are trash material.

Thus, to ease the burden, companies often resort to setting a high bar (no matter how impractical) so that most applicants will voluntarily self-select themselves out of this competition. If reading such a job application shakes your confidence, that's precisely what they want. They want fewer candidates to apply for this job. This substantially reduces the number of applicants they need to scrutinize. Did you notice how this sounded absurd to you (before knowing the context) but actually makes a lot of sense from the company's perspective?

The biggest mistake you can make in this context is to self-select yourself out of the game. Don't take the job requirements list to heart. Remember, it's just a wish list. If this is a job you really want to do and can do, by all means, apply. Go for it even if your profile barely matches the requirements. Chances are nobody's did. Hirers don't expect any exact matches either. Matter of fact, they'll compromise on their expectations as they already know they've set a high bar. Also considering that only fewer candidates will apply, you're more likely to land this job than others.

So, the next time you see unrealistic job requirements, get motivated to apply.

The Role of Social Media

This can never be understated. Today, we live in an age where anybody can look up anybody else online. This means your potential employer is likely to land on your social media profile. When this happens, they begin judging you based on it.

Employers use your professional social media page (such as LinkedIn) primarily to understand your skill set and achievements. If you own a professional website, and showcase your achievements there, it puts an even better impression. If you don't own a professional website, you should seriously consider getting one. It will increase your chances of getting hired multifold. Of course, if you can't, it's not a deal-breaker. Your LinkedIn page will do handsomely.

In these places, you want to demonstrate your proficiency in your core skill. For instance, if you're a software designer, your core skill is design. You want to showcase your best design creations in your website and professional social media. This will give employers a clear idea of what you can do for them.

While you're at it, also showcase your additional skills and interests. As a software designer, if you can do some level of software development as well, you should mention that. This makes employers think that, in addition to design, you can be assigned to do software development in a pinch. This makes your profile more valuable. If you have ever attended some type of designers' conference (whether or not it's any good), you should mention that. Such extracurricular activities show that you're personally interested in the work that you do.

With the above techniques, your profile becomes favorable both ways. For employers placing more value on your core skill, you've displayed it. For employers wanting to know if you're an all-round individual, you've shown that also.

On the other side of this equation lie personal social media. These include Facebook, X (formerly, Twitter), your personal blog and the like. These are sites where you post your personal opinions, photos etc. and share interesting posts.

That photo of your face smeared with birthday cake from two years ago forms an impression of you. That insulting comment you left a decade ago on a random post you don't even remember... yep, they've duly noted that. Employers can see who you're friends with, which pages or groups you like and what your true interests are.

Obviously, don't post anything obscene in these places. In the same vein, also stay away from topics like religion, politics, sensitive social issues, things considered taboo, crime or any other topic involving strong feelings or controversy. When posted, these topics have the potential to ruin your career.

Imagine a potential boss coming across these posts and they don't agree with you. They could be hurt by your post, even if you never meant to. If your post is about a topic that your hirer deeply cares about, he or she may be personally offended. Forget being rejected, there are worse outcomes. They may start holding a grudge on you, hire you at first and make your life miserable later on. If not, imagine someone in your friend list you added long ago and forgot all about. They may one day end up becoming your boss, subordinate or coworker and "avenge" the "atrocity" of this post. Yes, this is silly, uncivilized and borderline psycho behavior, but happens all the same.

On the contrary, sharing inoffensively funny, interesting, eye candy and educational posts will make you look like an interesting candidate. Posting about topics everybody would benefit from makes you look knowledgeable and tasteful while still signaling that you're not into controversial and toxic posts.

All in all, social media profiles play an important role in an employer's decision to hire you. We no longer live in an era where your resume and behavior during the interview alone matter. This is an era where your online presence speaks louder than your physical presence. It's imperative that we take advantage of social media to make a positive impression. If done right, social media profiles can be a huge boost to your candidacy.

First Impression Is the Only Impression

By now, you would've understood that employers judge candidates in many ways. Much of these ways are beyond our control. You get only one chance with most recruiters and your first impression is going to stay put like a tattoo. Most employers aren't open enough (and frankly, they don't have enough time) to give you a second chance. It's also impossible to make a good impression at every single place you go. So, if you happen to make a bad impression despite trying not to, skip that place and go somewhere else.

Remember that there will always be at least one negative employer who sees everything in a negative light. Do yourself a favor and walk right out of there.

You'll also come across umpteen positive and neutral employers who'll give you a fair chance. I suggest you focus your efforts more on them.

There's no saying how a given employer chooses to judge you. They can judge in any way they want. But there is something you can do that's very much within your control. You can make sure that any fair conclusions they draw from your words and actions can only be positive. You can see to it that you don't give them a chance to suppose anything negative about you. This way, you can lower your chance of failure as much as possible.

Creating the best first impression is a tricky process. It takes a lot of practice and patience. While it's not a guarantee, it can be achieved if you commit yourself to it. Always put your best foot forward. With the tips we have discussed so far, you can confidently present yourself as a highly desirable candidate to your potential employers. Good luck!

Chapter 5
50+ Interview Questions Answered

This chapter is the meat of this book. Answering interview questions is the core of giving job interviews. This is such a basic skill that every interviewee has to get right. Fortunately, here is a list of the most common interview questions with best or example answers along with additional info.

Question 1
Tell me about yourself.

Alternative Wording (Variants):
Introduce yourself.
Take me through your resume.
Give me a rundown/summary of your resume.
What is your past work experience like?

Why They Ask This Question
If you ask me, there are umpteen other better ways to start an interview. However, many interviewers don't have time to think of a better opening and, thus, resort to this boring question just because it's easier. This question is so open-ended that many candidates are confused about where to begin. Many often feel the pressure right at the start of an interview.

Whenever you hear this question, understand it as "what benefit do you bring to the company?" This benefit is also called "value". Always talk about how much you have understood the role in question and in what way you meet the requirements. Interviewers want to know exactly this and simply love candidates that directly answer this.

Ideal Answer

I am a [insert profession here]. I have experience working as a [position] for [number] of years. As you can see from my resume, I majored in [related education specialization] and I have worked for organizations like [company name], [company name] and [company name] as a [related position(s)].

I am very good at [task 1], [task 2] and [task 3]. In my experience, I have handled such tasks on a daily/frequent basis including challenges/additional requirements such as [challenge 1], [challenge 2] and [challenge 3]. From your ad, I understand you want your candidate to be/have [requirement 1], [requirement 2] and [requirement 3]. As you can see, my qualifications and experience match perfectly with these requirements. This is what brings me here today.

How to Say It

Practice saying this in front of a mirror (for a few days) to the point that you sound natural, confident and without stutter. Smile slightly as you say it (don't beam). Very importantly, keep this whole explanation to within one minute. Mention everything in a matter-of-fact tone rather than as a memorized announcement.

Only include qualifications and experience relevant to that job in particular. Modify the given script as you need. In case you seek a career change, mention at least one or two transferable skills from your current line of work, one pertinent educational qualification, one certified private course you attended in the new field, one internship or one volunteering activity related to the new line of work during the interview.

Why This Answer Works

This question is often intended to eliminate candidates. Recruiters are not going to like candidates who are unprepared for this question and fumble. It's quite possible that a recruiter might reject you solely based on this question. If you don't make sense in the first few sentences for this question, you might be out.

Interviewers typically look for answers to whether you're serious about this job, if you have given enough thought about the requirements and challenges as well as how you've planned to carry out your daily responsibilities.

This answer works because it not only details what is on your resume, which is the direct answer to the question, but also tells how it connects with the job requirements posted by the employer themselves, which is the true intended question.

63

Question 2

Why should we hire you?

Alternative Wording (Variants):

What makes you unique?

What can you do for us that some else can't?

Why are you the best candidate?

What will you contribute to the company?

What do you bring to the table?

In what way will you be an asset to the company?

Why would you be a good fit for this position?

How productive will you be at your work?

Why They Ask This Question

The actual question is "Why should we hire you in particular over everybody else who's competing for the same position?" The interviewer's job is precisely to figure this part out. It doesn't feel very good when they ask this to us so directly, but look at the flipside – this is a great opportunity to advertise all your strengths.

You best think beforehand about what makes you truly unique for that position. If you think hard, there should be at least one quality that you have that's quantifiably better than others. Quantifiable is the keyword here. If you still couldn't think of anything, just mention each job requirement and how you'll fulfill it. Make sure the answer is not a repetition of the answer to "Tell me about yourself".

Ideal Answer

I am glad you asked. You had said in your ad that you want someone with [number] years of experience, right? I have [greater number]. You said you want an undergraduate degree holder in this field, right? I am a post grad. Furthermore, I have made X, Y, Z achievements in my previous organizations. I have received awards/promotions/client appreciation e-mails purely for my quality of work and commitment to the role (briefly elaborate on one or two of the achievements). All in all, I am sure I could bring immense value to this organization.

(Make sure you bring the printed copy of the client appreciation e-mails and photos of receiving the awards, if applicable. This will boost your impression by a million times.)

How to Say It

Make sure your tone doesn't sound like bragging but still conveys the importance of your achievements in a factual way.

Why This Answer Works

This question often comes up when interviewers see the same things mentioned across several resumes. It's possible that the interviewer is at a loss to decide who the better candidate is. If anything, this is your chance to jump in as one of the first candidates and show your best side.

You need to talk about your strengths in such a way that sounds alluring to the interviewer. These strengths might be ones several others have and need not even be unique to you necessarily. However, the way in which you say it must make them say inside "Yes, yes! That's exactly what we want." The given answer does all this.

Question 3

Why do you want this job?

Alternative Wording (Variants):

Why do you want this role/position?

Why did you apply for this job?

What do you look for in a job/in this job?

How do you see this job as a step in your career?

What do you find most attractive about this position?

What do you expect from this new position?

Do you feel you are overqualified for this job?

Why They Ask This Question

The answer is obviously the money, to pay your bills. You can't say that in an interview, now, can you?

The interviewer is trying to understand if you have randomly sent out applications to any open job there is or whether you have applied to this job with enough forethought. Whatever you answer, never mention money or material benefits you get from the job. Instead, highlight how getting such a job will put your knowledge and skills to good use. Mention all the areas or tasks within this job that you'll excel in.

Ideal Answer

I have always wanted a job involving [requirement 1], [requirement 2], and [requirement 3]. These are my favorite types of work to do. This way, I get to exercise many of my skills such as [skill 1], [skill 2], and [skill 3] and put all my experience to good use. Thus, this job stood out as the ideal opportunity for me.

How to Say It

The way in which you say it should make it look like you're passionate about this job, preferably, without using the word "passion". Show genuine excitement for the work itself rather than the rewards. Also, keep the answer short.

Why This Answer Works

The interviewer wants to know if you'll stay in this job for a long time or leave too soon. If you answer money or other material benefits, it signals that you'll leave once you get a better pay elsewhere. Contrarily, if you answer that you enjoy the job itself, the employer will see it as a positive. This way, they need not worry about keeping you motivated. An already happy employee means more productivity with less maintenance.

The given answer highlights the job requirements, your suitability and your passion for performing on the role all in one go. At the same time, it also removes the focus from you and puts it on the job itself pretty smoothly.

Question 4

Why do you want to work in this company?

Alternative Wording (Variants):

What do you know about this company?

What interests you the most about our company?

How did you end up choosing this company?

Don't you think you might be better suited for a different type of company?

If you could choose any company, where would you go?

I see that you come from a prestigious company like X. Why would you leave your job there and come to work somewhere like here?

Why They Ask This Question

They want to know if you've evaluated their company well just like they're evaluating you. If you've selected this company consciously over others, then you're far more likely to stick to this company after joining. So, you want to demonstrate this in your answer even if the opposite is the case.

Please note that some of the variants above are trap questions. Don't fall for them. The answer is always this company.

Do your due diligent research about this company, namely what they do, which industry they're in, who their competitors are and how they stand out from the competition. Extra points if you can memorize and repeat the mission statements of the company from their website or brochure. While you're there, you can also read up on some company history.

Again, never mention material benefits given by the organization.

Ideal Answer

I want to work here because I heard nothing but good things about this company. I understand that the company is into such-and-such a business in this particular industry. This organization is a significant player in the market giving a tough competition to other companies like A, B and C. I went through the company website and found that the core values are X, Y and Z. These align well with my personal values in life. I believe this organization supports its employees in many ways and also provides a lot of growth opportunities. I feel my knowledge and skill set will be put to good use here.

(Make sure all your information about the industry and product portfolio is correct. Have one or two confirmed examples ready for how the organization supports its employees or provides opportunities.)

Never Say

Don't ever say you want to work for them because of salary, overtime benefits, lower work duration, promotion, leave policy, medical benefits, reimbursement benefits, extracurricular activities or even free lunch. This will make you look cheap and selfish.

How to Say It

Say it like you mean it. Say that you want to work in this industry and for a prestigious organization like them. Show that you've actually researched this company especially in terms of what it would be like working here. Mention examples such as training programs, mentorship systems, networking opportunities, research projects, freedom to experiment, awards for best performance, equal and fair treatment of employees, good communication practices etc. You should have confirmed that they do in fact give these opportunities. Mostly, you can find these things in the company website, employer review sites or by interacting with past employees. Don't mention any past or present employee's name during the interview. It's a strict no-no. The only exception to this rule is if that employee has officially recommended you.

Why This Answer Works

The given answer works because by mentioning information about the industry, the company's core activity or products, and company values, you're showing that you have put in your fair share of thought about joining this company. By mentioning actual opportunities, you're giving the impression that you have done your research.

Question 5

Why are you leaving your current job?

Alternative Wording (Variants):

Why are you changing jobs?

Why are you looking for a new job?

In your current (last) position, which things do (did) you like the most?

What do you think of your current (former) boss?

What do you like least about your current (last) job?

What are your pet peeves?

Why They Ask This Question

The interviewer is trying to see if you badmouth your previous company or boss. If you do, you'll also badmouth this company and job after you leave. They also want to know if you'll leave this job for similar reasons as your previous job. While making sure to not badmouth, you also need to give a convincing answer. Find out what this company or type of job offers better than the previous and say it in a way that is acceptable.

Ideal Answer

When it comes to my previous job, I am quite grateful to the organization for giving me the opportunity. It was a great experience working for them. I had a wonderful boss with kind coworkers. We, as a team, made so many achievements. I also left on good terms. Now, I am ready to do more. I feel like taking on a new challenge, working in a new company, a new position where I can learn more and contribute more. I am positive that this company and this position will be the right step in my career right now. I am excited about the opportunity to contribute to the team and help achieve the company's goals.

Never Say

Preferably, never say the actual reason you left. You don't want to, even in the smallest way, be negative about your previous employer.

How to Say It

Show gratitude in your tone as you thank your previous employer. Keep it short and quickly shift the focus on to this job. Stop talking afterwards. The silence will likely force your interviewer to move on to the next question.

Why This Answer Works

This answer begins with saying nice things about your past employer, which puts the interviewer at ease. It also avoids the real reason, which you don't want to say anyway. It focuses more on how you see this job. This answer shows you're enthusiastic to take up challenges in this job as well as meet with a new environment and people. All of this creates a positive impression of you.

Question 6

What's your expected salary?

Alternative Wording (Variants):

What's your current salary?

Why They Ask This Question and How to Answer

Fortunately, this is one of those questions that means exactly what it asks. Nevertheless, answering it requires some prep. Before the interview, you should go online to learn the going rates for your position and industry. You should also find out what this company pays. In addition to online, you can ask former employees of the company or anyone who works in the industry. If you feel this company pays too low, you should not be applying in the first place.

During the interview, note if they're asking this salary question at the very beginning of the interview process – in the first round or as one of the first questions. If yes, it could be an elimination question (trap). Companies hate good negotiators and will reject you if you show any hint of asking for a higher salary. You want to say something like "I want to know more about this job before I can tell you my expected salary" and skip the question for that time. If they press you more, ask "What's your allotted budget for this position?" Failing this, give a wide range that brackets the going market rate for this role as well as what the company usually pays.

If they're asking you later on in the process, with the intent of actually employing you, this is when you want to slowly start negotiating. Even then, don't give out a single number. Give them a reasonable range that's both within the company's pay scale and what you should be fairly paid. To know what you should be paid, take your past experience, qualifications and skill set as bases. If you've made a good impression, they might actually consider accommodating your expected salary.

Never Say

You should never let them know the exact number you have in mind. Especially toward the beginning of the interview, never tell or even hint at your expected salary – try to avoid it. If you can't avoid it, give a range.

How to Say It

Be confident when both skipping the question at first and actually mentioning your expectations later on. Show that you've researched the market and the company. Any sign of self-doubt would mean that the interviewer can negotiate you down to peanuts. At the same time, don't be too aggressive or hint any disrespect even if the interviewer is disrespectful. This could put a bad impression on you. Some interviewers are known to tell on you to their contacts at other companies. You may be surprised who's connected to whom. Thus, it's better to keep up your politeness.

Why This Answer Works

Avoiding this question in the beginning works because it allows the employer to see you as more than just a monthly expense in the company's account. It gives them a chance to evaluate your competencies *before* thinking of your salary. This means you'll stay longer in the interview process, giving you more opportunities to make a good impression. Also, giving a range shows you're flexible. Delaying the negotiation until they're close to choosing you increases the chances of getting your desired salary.

Question 7

Tell me your weakness.

Alternative Wording (Variants):

Tell me about a time you made a mistake.

Tell me about a time you failed.

Tell me one more weakness.

Why They Ask This Question

Ah, the dreaded weakness question! Don't you just hate it when they suddenly whip out this dangerous weapon? Interviewers usually test your confidence with this question. This is usually intended as an elimination game. More often than not, many candidates help eliminate themselves with this question. Thus, obviously, don't give out your real weakness. The employer is not interested in knowing that.

Give a safe weakness answer that's either completely unrelated to this job or something an employer wouldn't mind. It can even be one that's a boon in disguise for this job in particular. There's no fixed answer to this question. Think long and hard and come up with a safe weakness relevant to your industry and role. Make sure you mention this weakness as a consequence of something positive. This makes the weakness look less negative. Also mention that you have a way to fix this. This is important. You should be prepared if they ask for more than one weakness. So, have at least two weaknesses prepared.

Instead of directly asking for your weakness, if they start the question with "Tell me a time when...", they're expecting you to narrate an incident. So, just turn your weakness into an example incident.

Example Answer 1 (Weakness as a Consequence of a Positive Attribute)

I love taking on responsibilities and making sure they're fulfilled to the best level. Responsibilities make me feel good and give me a sense of purpose. However, sometimes, I do tend to take up more obligations than normal and end up forgetting a few details. To fix this, I started making a list of responsibilities I currently have. Once I started keeping lists, I've never forgotten even a single detail.

Example Answer 2 (Weakness or Mistake as a Past Incident)

I enjoy taking up meticulous work. Doing a task that includes lots of minute details gives me a sense of challenge and satisfaction. This is why, in my previous job, I was given the task of scheduling meetings between clients and company employees. There were various time slots and rooms. There may be changes in the meeting time or meeting room number at any time, even just before the start of a meeting. It's part of my job to accommodate these last-minute changes. It's easy to lose track even if there was just a moment's inattention. That's exactly what happened once. I mixed up a meeting with another as they sounded similar. Then, my boss suggested using only the company's scheduling software for all time-change or venue-change requests. After I did this, I've never faced this problem again.

Example Answer 3 (When Applying for a Traveling Salesman's Job)

I love socializing. I always start a conversation with somebody around me, even with strangers sitting next to me. I love to explain things a lot and, because of this, I have been able to win a huge customer base for my previous company. While this has never been a problem for me in my work, sometimes, in personal social situations, people around me said I might come off as a chatterbox because of the explaining. Since I received that feedback, I made sure I kept my personal conversations shorter but still interesting. After this, nobody said anything negative but started appreciating my social skills.

(Traveling salesmen are supposed to be chatterboxes to an extent. While tending to talk a lot might be a negative for an office job, for a travelling salesman, this might be seen as a plus.)

Example Answer 4 (When Applying for a Proofreader's Job)

I want to make sure there are no mistakes when I communicate whether orally or in writing. Thus, whenever I made spelling or grammar mistakes, I felt too bad. I started beating myself up on the inside, thinking that others will point out my spelling or grammar mistakes and make fun of it. Then, my colleague said except for the documents we proofread, nobody really cares about spelling or grammar in real life. The message we are trying to convey is way more important. So, in areas outside of work, I stopped being too strict with grammar while still making sure the message is clear.

(Proofreaders are expected to be sticklers for spelling and grammar errors. This is in fact a strength in disguise.)

Never Say

Never try to blatantly dress up an obvious strength as a weakness. Employers can see through it. However, you can mention something that definitely is a weakness in a general situation, but is somehow a strength to the role you are interviewing for (Examples 3 and 4). Make sure your weakness is true at least at some level. You don't want to completely fake it. Also, don't mention the word "weakness" in your answer.

How to Say It

Keep it short. Don't go into explaining your weakness and making it look bigger than it is. Be confident as you answer this question. Put a positive spin on it. The best way to do this is to mention your weakness as an unintended consequence of a strength. When you say this, also mention that you have identified your weakness and took steps to correct. You want to practice saying this in front of a mirror multiple times before the interview.

Why These Answers Work

The given answers all begin with a good attribute about you. They start out positively (shows confidence). Later on, they mention the resulting negative without using the word "weakness". All the answers also show that you've taken steps to correct the issue such that it's no problem at all in the present.

Question 8

Tell me your strengths.

Alternative Wording (Variants):

What are your most positive attributes?

What are your specialties or strong suits?

Why They Ask This Question

In contrast to the weakness question, you might think this is a safe question to answer. In reality, this question is also a pitfall. There are many ways in which the interviewer can reject you here! If you start speaking too much about your strengths, you come off as too much of a braggart. If you don't state your strengths enough, the interviewer may not register it at all. See the catch-22 here?

In addition, the employer is not interested in knowing any strength other than those that directly relate to this job. If your strength isn't going to make you work better than others, don't say it. Also, what you mention as strength may not be perceived as such by the interviewer. It helps to be aware of what that interviewer thinks is a strength. You can get this from the job description.

So, the safest way to answer this question is to stick with whatever job requirements the company has posted. Just mention each requirement you meet as your strength (you need not necessarily meet all requirements). Make sure your answer is not a verbatim repetition of the answers to

"Tell me about yourself" or "Why should we hire you" questions. Paraphrase the same content though.

Example Answer

When it comes to this job, my biggest strengths are [job requirement 1], [job requirement 2] and [job requirement 3]. I have ample practice doing [job requirement 1] because, in my previous workplace, I had to do [related example activity] every day. It was an enjoyable challenge. [Job requirement 2] is a valuable skill that I feel will help me finish this job quicker while still giving quality. I was trained in [job requirement 3] back in college as part of [class name] class. Overall, I believe these strengths will help me carry out this job with effectiveness and efficiency.

(Tweak this answer as you need.)

Never Say

Absolutely no bragging in the slightest. Also, don't list too many strengths. The ideal number is three and the minimum number I'd recommend is two. Don't speak more than one or two sentences about each strength.

How to Say It

Say it in a confident but not cocky tone. Be matter of fact about the strengths and their connection to this job. When you pick your strengths right from the job description, make sure it doesn't seem obvious you picked it from there. That is to say, describe it in your own words.

Specifically describe how the strengths relate to this job, so that the answer feels fuller.

Why This Answer Works

This answer works because it answers the question directly, while still avoiding the double bind. Interviewers will like this answer because it ties back to the requirements.

Question 9

Where do you see yourself in 5 years from now?

Alternative Wording (Variants):

What are your long-term goals?

What are your career aspirations?

What is your dream job?

What does success look like to you?

How would you define success?

How long will you stay with us?

Why They Ask This Question

The future is uncertain for all of us. It's very hard to say what we'll do next week, let alone the next five years. For all you know, the interviewer themselves have no idea what they'll do in the next five years. Having said all this, there's a reason they ask this.

The interviewer is probing to see how long you've planned to stay in this position. They want to hear you say you'll stay in this job five years later doing this very work. Interviewers hate candidates who have promotion in their mind. However, saying so directly also means you have no long-term ambitions. Answering this directly is a problem both ways.

Ideal Answer

This job is something I've always wanted to do in my life. I enjoy this line of work. To me success means achieving the targets set forward by my manager and organization to the best of my ability. In five years (or for the foreseeable future), I see myself in this team, becoming a high-performing and productive member of the team. I'll become a reliable worker for the team. You can count on me for completing tasks within time and to a high standard. I am also open to any decision the management might make regarding my future in this company after reviewing my work.

Never Say

Saying anything like you see yourself in another position or company is going to reject you straightaway. Don't act smart and say things like "I want to be in your position", "I'll become the CEO" etc. In fact, don't answer with anything besides the position you've applied for.

How to Say It

Say it confidently with enthusiasm like you mean it. Keep it short. Smile.

Why This Answer Works

The given answer puts the interviewer at ease by saying that you'll be a highly productive and reliable team player. These will usually be the immediate concerns of any interviewer. Likewise, the answer also says you'll accept any decision they make about you. This shows you'll be cooperative and easygoing. This way, the interviewer can neither reject you for wanting a higher position nor for lack of ambition.

Question 10

How do you plan on achieving those aforementioned goals?

Alternative Wording (Variants):

Your goals are too general.
Your goals are unrealistic.
You call that a goal?

Why They Ask This Question

The interviewer is trying to see if you're serious about your long-term goals. They are checking if you have an actual plan to achieve them. By commenting that your goals are not good enough, the interviewer is trying to check your confidence. This is another elimination question. They will note if you get defensive or irritated at such a direct negative remark on your goals.

While "how you plan to achieve" is something you can answer with relative ease, the others (variants) are a type of stress interview question. If the latter happens, you want to evaluate if you want to continue the interview, and if you do, it's best to keep your cool while thinking of an answer.

Ideal Answer

I plan to achieve those goals by hard work, commitment to the process and being consistent at my work. My goal may seem general to you, because I have made it flexible enough to include all possible scenarios. I don't see anything wrong or unrealistic about wanting to be high-performing and productive.

Never Say

Don't get angry or lose your cool. Keep smiling and keep your tone calm. Don't try to mock the interviewer or criticize the question. Make sure your answer doesn't come off as defensive or as a result of provocation. If you feel the interviewer is being unbearably brutal, walk out of the room and out of the building. You don't want such a job anyway. There's no use of shouting at or fighting with an interviewer.

How to Say It

Keep your tone normal as it would be for other questions. Smile.

Why This Answer Works

This answer focuses on answering the question without getting emotional. It shows confidence despite negativity. It shows you'll not change your goals for anybody or anything while still being respectful.

Question 11

Which other companies have you applied to?

Alternative Wording (Variants):

What career options do you have at this moment?
If you had to change your career right now, which career would you choose?
Describe a recent job interview experience you have had.

Why They Ask This Question

The interviewer wants to know if you have options.

Most career advisers would suggest that you say you *are* interviewing with other companies. They say it makes you look like a more in-demand employee. The logic here is the interviewer might quote a higher salary when offering you the job. Sure, this would be true in a market where employees are more in demand and less in supply. In such a market, employees will have more negotiation power. If you know for a fact that your field has more demand and less supply, you can mention that you're interviewing with other companies.

However, in the present day and age, the opposite is true. Hundreds or even thousands of applicants for a single opening is nothing to be surprised about. In this situation, if an employer gets to know that you have options, they'd save themselves the hassle of negotiating with you. They'd rather reject you straightaway, pick up the next application and give that person a shot.

Thus, a better strategy, in most cases, is to actually say you're not interviewing with anybody else.

Ideal Answer

I started searching for a job and your ad immediately caught my eye. I have always wanted to work in a role where [job requirement 1], [job requirement 2] and [job requirement 3] would be part of the work. So, your job posting stood out to me as an ideal choice. I immediately applied and got the interview call. I thought let me attend this one first and see where it takes me. Here I am.

Never Say

The worst way to bungle up this question is to mention the names of the other companies you're interviewing with. Forget the interviewer thinking you may negotiate more – some HR or hiring managers are known to call up that other company and sabotage your chances there. You have no idea who's connected to whom and what type of strings they can pull.

Your best bet is to say you're interviewing only here, no matter how much they force you.

How to Say It

Sound happy that you found this job posting. Show excitement when talking about the job requirements and responsibilities. Show how passionate you are about them.

Why This Answer Works

Answering this way removes the focus from you or other companies and puts it back on this job. It shows you're giving more importance to this job and company than any other. You're already excited about the job requirements, which comes off as a positive. With this answer, you have also subtly praised the job posting, which, if the interviewer was involved in designing or posting, would make them feel good at a personal level.

Question 12

Why is there a gap in your employment?

Alternative Wording (Variants):

Why haven't you found a job before now?

Why They Ask This Question

This is another question that actually means what they ask. An applicant with a long work gap means they are not serious about this job or having a job in general. You must say you are in fact serious about taking up a job, and this gap is an unfortunate one-off incident.

While there are no hidden meanings here, the answer you give is very important. It might make or break the interview. Some companies have a strict policy against hiring employees with work gaps. For instance, if they ask this question over the phone or before the interview, they may be looking for a chance to reject you. On the other hand, if they are asking this question after having called you in for an interview, that means they're willing to give you a chance to explain yourself. If they ask this at a much later stage in the hiring process, then, probably, they're willing to look past your work gap.

The best way to hide work gaps is to be proactive and take up a volunteering activity (community service), freelance gig or even an educational course during that gap. This should have been planned and executed beforehand. In case you didn't, there are still other valid reasons you can say such as taking care of kids, tending to a sick family member, helping out a friend or relative during a difficult situation, you planned for a grad course that didn't work out and so on.

Example Answer 1

During those years, I really wanted to get into a job much like this one. At the same time, I had a family member (parent/spouse/child) who fell sick. There was no one except me to constantly care for their ailment, accompany them to the hospital, cook and clean for them and give them medication on time. When the choice is between my job and their well being, I had to choose them. After giving enough care and treatment, they have completely recovered now. So, I am ready to commit to your organization and in this role.

Example Answer 2

I had been working as a [insert position here] for several years. I had made several achievements during that time as you can see from my resume. Then, we had kids. Since my spouse could not leave their job, and we had no one else to safely hand kids over to, I decided to take time off and take care of them. At present, my kids are all grown up and can take care of themselves. I can now fully devote myself to your company and this role.

Example Answer 3

After my years of work at [company name], and before taking up my next employment, I felt it was time to take a break to enhance my skills. So, I enrolled into a [course name] course with [institution name]. They trained me well in [skill 1], [skill 2] and [skill 3]. In the evenings, I also did community service for [name of nonprofit organization]. Here are my certificates for both.

(Obviously, you must have planned this ahead and have certificates ready)

Example Answer 4

I was working as a software developer. Between that job and the next, I used the time to finish my personal software project that I had always been meaning to do. This project is about a billing system for supermarkets that also doubles up as a stock-keeping system and cash flow tracker. The project is now completely finished, and I am fully ready to work for you.

(Have a sample of the project ready to show, if possible. This will show that you're truly passionate about the work and are keeping in touch with your skills even during unemployment.)

Never Say

Saying you could not get a job (no matter the reason) is a strict no-no. Also, don't say things like the economy was bad etc. Never blame the industry or companies. Never, directly or indirectly, say you enjoyed the work gap. Enjoying not having any work means you're lazy. Show that the work gap was either a self-improvement experience or you did something productive and necessary during that time.

How to Say It

Never show any sign of guilt as you express yourself. Interviewers may subconsciously detect this and strike off your name. Show that the work gap was more of a deliberate choice than otherwise. Keep it short. One or two explanatory sentences are usually enough. Soon after, drive the conversation back to how you fit the job requirements.

Why These Answers Work

These answers work because there's nothing negative about the given reasons, and you're unlikely to get rejected for these in a fair situation. Taking care of family is always a valid reason to have work gaps. Showing you've been productive during work gaps will create an impression that you're an active and hardworking person. Volunteering means you're ready to work even with little to no monetary rewards. If the employer has already considered your other positive attributes, they will easily accept these reasons and move on.

Question 13

Can you explain why you changed or want to change career paths?

Alternative Wording (Variants):

What prompted your career change?
Why are you seeking a different career now?
How long have you been considering this career change?
How do you plan to address any skill gaps you may have because of this career change?

Why They Ask This Question

This is a very different question from "Why do you want this job?" or "Why are you leaving your current job?" Here the fact that you're changing the very nature of your job is being questioned. They'll usually ask this question if this is the first job you're applying to after choosing the new career or if you have changed careers after being in one career for a long time. In any case, career change involves starting afresh and learning everything about the new field from the ground up.

The interviewer is trying to check whether you understand all the challenges that come with this. You will likely start from an entry-level position and, typically, your current work experience will not be considered. Your salary may also be regressed to the lowest. Essentially, the interviewer asks what made you press the reset button on your career.

To convince the interviewer, tell them a safe reason for career change. Some safe reasons include seeking a new challenge, wanting a change, personal interests and values, health and gaining experience. While you're at it, highlight the transferable skills, if any, that will count toward this job.

No negative answers, badmouthing people or discrediting the previous career.

Ideal Answer

I thoroughly enjoyed working in my previous career. I learned so much and my experience there has made me an adept employee in the field. I made so many achievements in that field as you can see from my resume. After all these years, I now feel a need to move on. I feel my skill set can be put to better use in a field like this one. I have always wanted to work in a job where skills like [job requirement 1], [job requirement 2] and [job requirement 3] are required. I am sure everything I learned in the previous career is going to come in handy for this job also. Many of the skills such as [skill 1], [skill 2] and [skill 3] are transferrable. To prepare for this role and industry, I have finished several private courses and internships. I also read several books such as [book 1], [book 2] and [book 3] to understand the technicalities. All in all, I am eager to start working here.

(Show certificates for private courses and internships.)

<u>Never Say</u>

Obviously, never mention the problems you had in your past career. Don't say bad boss, bad coworkers, low salary, no stability, no work-life balance, no advancement, too many expectations etc. Don't complain. Paint a positive picture about your past career, the reason for leaving and why you chose this career.

<u>How to Say It</u>

Show calm happiness when talking about your previous career and all the companies that you worked for. Keep it short and stop talking afterwards. Whatever you do, don't feel the need to justify or to fill any silences. No matter how awkward the silence is, wait for your interviewer to move on to the next question.

<u>Why This Answer Works</u>

This answer begins with saying nice things about your previous career, which implies you're not leaving because of any problems. The reason for moving on is also nothing to be alarmed about. It shows you are a challenge-lover and are ready to adapt to a new environment and a new type of work. If the interviewer follows up with something like "You will have to start from a lower position" etc., you have to be open to saying yes because this is a career change after all.

Question 14

If you could start your career over again, what would you do differently?

Alternative Wording (Variants):

How do you feel about your career journey?

How successful do you think you have been so far?

What are your biggest career regrets?

What are your biggest regrets in life?

What do you feel you have not achieved in your life till now?

Why They Ask This Question

This is another confidence tester. Some companies want to hire only those candidates who feel successful. While we all have best and worst things about our careers (or lives) and not all of us feel great about it, we are expected to put on a show as if we are proud about every single thing. A candidate with regrets or discontentment is a bad hire straightaway.

To answer this question, simply summarize the best moments (achievements) of your career and conclude. When they say "life", assume they mean your professional life. Your personal life is none of their business.

Ideal Answer

I feel very fortunate to have had an exciting and rewarding career as a [insert position here]. I began my career as a [entry level position] where I had the opportunity to take up the most challenging tasks straightaway. That company [company name] gave me complete freedom and support so that I can perform my work in the best way. I made several achievements there such as [achievement 1], [achievement 2] and [achievement 3]. I had great managers who were very easy to work with. Later on, I moved to [name of the next company], where once again I was gifted with a fantastic team. All my bosses and coworkers were nice. Here, I gained [number] years of experience working in [area of expertise or job requirement]. My achievements here include [achievement 1], [achievement 2] and [achievement 3]. [Mention further organizations and experiences].

Overall, I am very satisfied with my career. I consider my career as one of my blessings in life. If I could change anything about my career or life, I would not change a thing.

Never Say

Never say you would change something about your career. That means you have complaints or regrets, and the interviewer will reject you the moment they hear it. Remember, you feel delighted about your career journey and you've been mighty successful in it.

How to Say It

Be excited when this question is asked, but don't overdo it. Talk about all your accomplishments cheerfully. Mention all the people you have met (bosses, subordinates, coworkers) in a positive light. Don't mention anybody's name as you have no idea who is connected to whom and what they can snoop around about you.

Why This Answer Works

This answer works because you have essentially avoided the trap set by the interviewer. There is absolutely no reason to reject you here. Besides, you've mentioned all your past activities in a positive light. If anything, you have turned an attempt to reject you into an actual, valid reason to hire you.

Question 15

What is your greatest professional achievement?

Alternative Wording (Variants):

Tell me about a challenge or conflict you faced at work, and how you dealt with it.

Tell me about a time when you had to come up with an innovative solution to a problem.

Tell me about a time you demonstrated leadership skills.

Are you a good manager? Give examples.

Do you consider yourself a leader? If yes, what makes you think so?

Tell me another achievement.

Why They Ask This Question

An interviewer is more likely to ask this question for a management position or any higher-level position. To answer this question the best way possible, narrate an incident where you solved a problem, seized an exciting opportunity or made a crucial decision.

You have to come up with a sensible story – one that's relevant to your field, your position, your everyday tasks and what's practically possible. You want to start with reminding the interviewer what your daily work was in a previous organization. Then, elaborate on some sudden problem or opportunity that came up. Follow this with the solution or decision you implemented. This is called the three-act structure (the setup, the problem and the solution). Within your story, include how you convinced others, the challenges you faced while implementing and, most importantly, the <u>quantifiable</u> results your solution brought about.

The word quantifiable is the most important part. You can even start your story with a quantifiable fact before going into the details. Quantities help an interviewer understand the gravity of the situation you explain.

Definitely have more than one story in case they're not convinced and want another. The following example answers might help you come up with some.

<u>Example Answer 1</u>

In my previous role as a technical trainer, I increased the team efficiency by 25% especially during a severe staff shortage. This was during a time when several senior and experienced members of the team quit suddenly. We were facing an acute labor shortage. To add to this, we were seeing an unusually large volume of work being submitted to us. More work loaded upon fewer workers' backs – the pressure was very real.

I came forward and told my manager that I am ready to take up a larger-than-usual batch for training. I promised I'll bring them up to speed quickly. While the usual number of trainees in a batch would be kept to 10 or less (so that individual attention can be given), I was ready to take up 30.

I put in extra hard work and stayed back additional hours each day to make sure everybody got individual attention. In addition, I also set for myself a time frame of one month to finish the training. For context, the usual minimum time taken for training is three months. The organization had a very high standard for trainees to pass. So, every trainee has to be thoroughly trained without any flaw. By the end of the training, I couldn't believe what I saw. In that batch, more than 90% of the trainees passed the training! I was pleasantly surprised when most of them had made it.

When they got on the actual job, we finished all pending jobs in a jiffy. Then, we started clearing the current jobs at a faster-than-usual rate. Within a short time, we turned the tables almost seamlessly. By the end of it all, our team got so efficient that we were ready for even bigger work volumes.

Example Answer 2

Prior to applying here, I was working as a senior sales manager in X organization where I increased the sales by 150% while reducing costs by 50%. One fine quarter, the company's sales figures suddenly dipped due to several reasons – bad economy, price rise and shift in consumer preferences. Our company also faced a severe cash crunch at the same time. It was a particularly trying time for us. To bring down expenses, I suggested to the top management that we decrease spending on traditional marketing. My idea was to focus more on door-to-door sales. While the top management initially thought this was a risky move, they later agreed considering the cost savings.

We specifically targeted existing customers who may want to rebuy our product. Most of the existing customers repeated their purchase. We also focused on new prospects that looked promising. Since our brand name was already well known, new prospects were more willing than we thought.

In addition, we did Facebook campaigns, YouTube videos, cold calling, classified ads and whatever else we could without spending much. By the end of everything, we could show a 1.5 times or 150% increase in our sales figures. And, we pulled this off with only half the usual budget. For this achievement, the company awarded me "Best Manager of the Year" trophy.

Example Answer 3

At [company name] software company, I was the project manager. A high-profile client had a $2 million project to offer. We never worked with this client before but we heard great things about them. Not only can they pay well but this client could also bring us more projects in the future. So, winning this project became our top priority.

We arranged a meeting with the client and put our best foot forward. Despite our best efforts, they said they'll get back to us, but we heard nothing back from them. We were worried. Through a mutual contact, we got to know that the client wasn't convinced of our capabilities. Normally, we would've left it then and there. But this was high value. Bagging this deal was paramount.

During what felt like an impasse, I came up with the idea of offering them a free sample. I felt this should be convincing. This was a difficult move for many reasons. Firstly, if we approached this the wrong way, we could come off as desperate. Also, the sample itself is going to take time, money and effort to make. In case the client isn't convinced with the sample, all this would've been for nothing. We could lose a high-value client forever!

Despite the risks, we decided to give it a shot. We had a strong understanding of what the client wanted and perfect coordination between our team members. Within a week, we had a minimum viable sample that we could show them. When the client saw it, they were visibly impressed. You should've seen their faces. They were so happy. They scheduled a meeting with us the very next day and signed the contract on the spot. This client went on to become one of our company's long-term patrons. We have collaborated on a lot of interesting projects over the years.

Never Say

Never mention one of your daily tasks as a challenge. This will significantly weaken your candidacy. Your challenge should be something out of the ordinary. Focus on what you in particular did to solve it.

How to Say It

Take this as an opportunity to tell your exciting story. Describe what made the situation particularly difficult. Use the right emotions in your word choice and tone of voice to emphasize the struggles. Make it clear how your solution came about as a miracle that turned the situation around. As already mentioned, quantify the result so that they can clearly understand why this is a big deal.

Why Such Answers Work

Any answer you come up with based on the given examples is going to directly answer the question, which is good. This is because of the three-act structure. Also known as the setup-problem-solution approach, this is an age-old technique used in movies, novels, TV shows etc. Any story narrated in this format is going to be exciting. Using this technique during the interview will clearly demonstrate how strong you can be during a tough situation. If done with due preparation, this answer could boost up your candidacy way above the competition.

Question 16

In your present (last) position, what problems did you identify that had previously been overlooked?

Alternative Wording (Variants):

What improvements did you bring to the day-to-day process in your organization?

Can you provide an example of when you showed initiative without anyone prompting you?

Do you have top-management potential? Give examples.

Are you a self-starter?

Tell me something you did in your previous company/organization that demonstrated that you had the long-term welfare of the organization in mind.

This job requires you to be self-motivated. Are you?

Why They Ask This Question

This question may be common in some management position interviews. The interviewer wants to know whether you went above and beyond the call of duty in your previous role. They're testing whether you took so much personal interest that you improved something that was already working well. They expect you to be vigilant about the everyday process itself. They want you to be a prevention-is-better-than-cure type of person. There are so many sub-points here.

This question has the potential to throw you off guard if you're not prepared. One more reason this is difficult because it tests your out-of-the-box thinking skills. In a typical management position, not everybody has the freedom or time to improve a process that's already working well. However, for the sake of this question, you should think of some answer that's true or at least borders on the truth.

The technique to answer this is very similar to the previous question, except that there is no challenge to be described here. So, come up with something that's appropriate to your position and line of work.

Example Answer 1

In my term as the team lead at [company name], I more than tripled the team's output with only a few simple changes. I was responsible for managing the [team name] team end to end, which consisted of [number] members and responsible for [core work of the team].

Our team was already one of the best performing teams in the company. However, the senior most members of our team felt that the job was not challenging anymore. This wasn't affecting our current output in any way at all. But I realized having dissatisfied employees, especially highly experienced ones, could affect our productivity later down the line.

I took this as an opportunity and made the senior members supervisors for the entire team. They'll assess the team's performance on a daily basis on top of their usual responsibilities. By doing this, the seniors felt challenged once again. They were happy. This change also massively eased my burden. My performance assessment became a weekly thing instead of the mandatory daily. I could then focus on other areas.

This one simple change alone was so effective that we had over three times more output than we did previously. This also successfully motivated the previously dissatisfied senior members and rekindled their morale.

Example Answer 2

As the general manager of such-and-such company dealing in [product name] products, I was responsible for showing increased sales every year. While our sales figures had been growing consistently, I had a feeling that there was more untapped potential.

I noticed that only 10% percent of the customers who showed interest in our products actually ended up buying. I felt the conversion rate could be improved. I realized customers were hesitant because ours was a relatively new brand. Having found this out, I felt the simplest solution was to hand out free samples. This way, the customers can get a feel of our product before making a decision.

This one change alone increased the conversion rate to 25% within a single month. The sales figures also improved accordingly. This became an important turning point in our company's sales history and is something I am very proud of.

Never Say

Don't say that you changed something because there was a problem. Remember, this question is about showing the thirst to improve without anybody or anything pushing you from behind. Talk about a situation where you prevented something negative from happening well before others even noticed. If not, think about a situation where you felt the existing process was wasting time, manpower or resources and could be improved.

How to Say It

Keep it simple. Keep it short. Mention only the necessary details. Quantify the result.

Why Such Answers Work

When you say you identified a potential opportunity or improved an existing process, it directly answers the question. It checks all the boxes including proactive, preventionist, self-motivated, focus on the big picture, top-management potential, selflessness and so much more.

Question 17

Tell me about a time you had a disagreement with your manager.

Alternative Wording (Variants):

Tell me about a time you had a conflict with your boss/subordinates/coworkers.

If we give you this job, tell me how you'll handle a given conflict?

Would you describe a few situations in which your work was criticized?

Why They Ask This Question

Everybody has disagreements with their bosses, subordinates or coworkers. There's nothing wrong with that as long as the end result improves the company's business and increases the profit. The interviewer wants to know if you disagreed amicably, whether you showed respect during the argument, whether or not you took it personally, what the communication style was like, whether the two of you solved it between yourselves and, most importantly, whether it affected your relationship negatively in any way.

Your answer must demonstrate that you showed professionalism during the conflict and your argument ultimately benefited the company.

A disagreement with a boss is considered more important than one with others. This is so because you need to respect authority. They want to know if you'll be disrespectful to your boss during a disagreement.

The given answer below is a specific example from an argument-with-boss perspective. You can adapt it for an argument with someone else and for your specific issue.

Example Answer

I usually don't disagree with my manager. I always make it a point to be obedient and cooperative. However, there was this one occasion where my boss wanted to implement a new software system that he believed would bring in more efficiency to the team. I took a look at the software and found out that it wasn't the best fit for our team. While my boss was enticed by the exciting new features of that software, I was more concerned about the high price we had to pay. I felt the existing software was already good enough and we only needed to make minor changes.

I respectfully shared my concerns with him and explained the merits of the software we already have. I told him that I appreciate his viewpoint and I'd love to have new exciting software too. However, the returns we may get from the new software won't even make back the money we invest. I provided ample data to support my argument and offered alternative solutions that I believed would be much more pocket friendly.

We sat down and had an effective discussion. In the end, my boss saw the truth in my argument and changed his mind. He later appreciated my efforts and told me that I did the right thing. From then on, we had a very productive relationship. This decision saved our company thousands of dollars in potential expenses.

Never Say

Never say you have never had an argument with your boss. The interviewer knows as well as you that that's a lie. Never ever say you had an argument with your boss about your salary, promotion or something else that you stand to gain personally or something that's not related to work. This will instantly reject you.

Also, don't blame your boss or criticize your boss or anybody else for the argument, even in passing. It's nobody's fault that you argued. Not even yours. You argued because you believed it'll benefit the company.

Nobody was right or wrong here. There's no me vs. them. You and your boss (or subordinates or coworkers) are all working in the same team for the same company. Don't openly say you were right and they were wrong. This makes you come off as inept and a hopeless egomaniac.

Likewise, use more positive or neutral-sounding words in your explanation. What you're describing is an already negative incident. Using negative words in addition will increase your chances of making a bad impression. Thus, even if the question uses words like argument, conflict, dispute, debate, disagreement, misunderstanding, criticism etc., don't use such words in your reply. Instead use words like discussion, conversation, talk, consultation, dialog, meeting, conference, chat etc.

Lastly, don't narrate more than one argument incident. The interviewer might think you argue a lot.

How to Say It

Be direct with the incident. Don't feel guilty for having had an argument. Don't feel uncomfortable answering this question. If you do these things, the interviewer will think you're hiding something or you had an argument for something you shouldn't have.

Mention valid reasons for why you chose to disagree. Compare and contrast both sides of the argument before revealing why you chose a particular side. Tell them you had no other choice but to disagree as the matter was important. Provide logical data points to support your position. While doing this, make sure your tone isn't accusatory. Mention your points as calmly and neutrally as possible.

Ideally, you want to say you convinced your boss or coworker successfully and prevented a potential mishap to the company. Also, make sure you clarify that you're usually very obedient to your boss, never argue, and this is a one-off incident.

Why This Answer Works

This answer makes neither you nor your boss look like the wrong side. This answer explains how you both were right in your own ways but ultimately did what was right for the company. Answering it this way shows that you were both respectful with each other, had open lines of communication and were logical in your decision-making process. Most importantly, the answer ends with how the relationship was never damaged despite the disagreement. This is something interviewers expect.

Question 18

Tell me a time when you had to make a difficult decision.

Alternative Wording (Variants):

What was the toughest decision you made?

Tell me about a time when you had to make a quick decision.

Tell me about a time you handled a difficult situation.

Tell me about a time when you had to think on your feet.

Why They Ask This Question

This question is similar to the question about your best achievement. The interviewer wants to know how you make decisions, what factors you consider, how you interact with people, and how you handle pressure.

To answer this question, you want to narrate an incident where you made a pivotal decision. While many experts say it's also okay to talk about a personal decision, I'd strongly urge you to keep it work related. After all, you want your interviewer to imagine you on the job, don't you? Besides, your personal life and the decisions you make in it are none of their business. If this is your first job and you're fresh out of college, you can talk about how you chose your college, your major or something about your study.

This is a very important question especially for a management role. So, it's crucial that you come up with a suitable incident well in advance before answering.

Example Answer 1

I was working at [company name] as the manager of the [team name] team. During a review, I had to promote one member from the team to a more senior role. I could easily narrow it down to two people. However, choosing one of them over the other was extremely difficult.

I relied purely on their merits, performance and job requirements. I wanted to make this as fair as possible. For a long time, the two candidates seemed equal in every metric. Then, for the umpteenth time, I took a look at the new position's job requirements. When analyzed closely, for one of the requirements, one candidate was slightly more fitting than the other. It was only by a small margin. However, since that requirement was very important, I made my decision using this metric.

After taking some time and considering everything, I chose that candidate. I called both of them separately into my room and had a frank discussion. I explained that only one person must be chosen and that I have been as objective as possible. The situation was very delicate. I told the unsuccessful candidate that I know how talented they are and the wealth of experience they have. I also added that if the next opportunity comes up, I'll seriously consider them. While that person was obviously disappointed, they agreed with me ultimately.

I made sure nobody had any long-term regrets over this issue.

Example Answer 2

During my time as the manager of software development, we had won a high-value contract. The payout of that single contract was equal to what the company would make from all other contracts combined. It was huge! The top management strongly hoped we'd bag this deal. When the client explained the project to us, it seemed like a very cut-and-dried task. Everybody from our team thought it was doable. Since the client wanted a quicker reply from us, we approved it. The deal was signed.

In the next few days, we began prototyping the project. This was when we realized this project was much bigger in scope than we initially thought. Doing such a project was way beyond our company's means. Of course, it came as a rude shock to the team. If we say we can't do this project now, the top management will think quite low of us. The client will be quite disappointed too. This was a tough spot to be in.

Despite the difficulty, I had to do what was best for the company. If we went forward with the project and failed later, it'd be an even bigger embarrassment. Therefore, I scheduled a meeting with the top management and explained everything. I told them that while this job's payout may be high, the costs will be even higher. That would be a net loss. I backed up all my calculations with appropriate statistics and client specifications. I explained that even if everyone in the company worked on this project, we could never complete it.

Initially, the top management was disappointed. Then, slowly, they understood the situation. They appreciated our team for noticing this beforehand. We scheduled another meeting with the client and explained all this. They were quite understanding as they already knew this was a difficult project. Ultimately, a lot of the company's time and money was saved.

Never Say

The worst way to fail this answer is to say you've never made a tough decision. This is especially true if you have done any type of management at all – even a small, temporary supervision role.

Never say someone else made the decision. They are asking about *your* decision-making skills here. Someone else could have given a suggestion, but you made the decision ultimately.

Also, never say it was your fault or anybody else's fault. However, do explain how and why the decision was tough to make.

Obviously, don't say your decision turned out to be bad or you were wrong about something in the end. You want to show that you make the right decisions.

How to Say It

Keep the incident short with only the most relevant details. Explain how the decision came up, the pros and cons of each choice, impact of the decision on the organization and how it ultimately saved the day. Subtly demonstrate that you showed diplomacy and emotional intelligence while handling the situation. This would go a long way.

Why Such Answers Work

The given answers clearly demonstrate all the ingredients interviewers expect in a decision-making story – the gravity of the situation, the parties involved, the factors considered, the consequences of each option, the ultimate decision, tactfulness and, most importantly, the final result of the decision.

Question 19

What is your strategy to handle stress?

Alternative Wording (Variants):

How well can you work under pressure?

How would you manage if the situation at work gets too challenging for you to handle?

How do you deal with emotional conflict?

How would you emotionally recharge yourself after a difficult situation at work?

Why They Ask This Question

They usually ask this question when the job you've applied for is known to be stressful. They want you to be prepared. If they ask you this question, evaluate if you're ready to handle a higher-than-ordinary amount of stress. If you feel you're not ready, leave the interview as soon as possible.

If you want this job and want to answer the question, the best strategy is to confidently say that you're very good at handling stress and remain silent afterwards. Wait for the interviewer to move on to the next question.

This is so because the moment you elaborate on this question, you'll have to talk about past things that stressed you. The more you talk about those things, the more you'll look like you can't handle stress. This in turn will put a bad impression on you no matter how well you say it. When you answer it with one line and stay silent thereafter, mostly the interviewer will move on to the next question.

If at all they dig you further, once again answer with only one or two sentences. Give a surface-level answer but avoid the question as such. Make sure your reply technically answers the question but doesn't go into details. However, if they ask for a specific incident from your past, look at the next question in this chapter.

Ideal Answer

Oh, I can handle stress very well. (Stay silent afterward).

Ideal Answer, if They Push You to Elaborate

Yes, I completely understand that workplace stress is an unavoidable situation. We all have to face it. But it has never been a problem for me in the past. (Stay silent afterward).

Ideal Answer, if They Ask Specific Strategies You Use to Handle Stress

Well, after work, I go to the gym. That takes care of the stress for me. (Stay silent afterward).

Ideal Answer, if They Ask for a Specific Incident from Your Past

See next question.

Never Say

Don't get put off by this question. Don't put on an uncomfortable face. Be comfortable in your body language and tone of voice as you answer this question.

Also, never say you'll never get stressed. The interviewer is no idiot. Never explain how emotionally draining a stressful incident could be. This will give the impression that you get emotionally affected. Interviewers don't want that. The point here is to show yourself as a tough cookie.

How to Say It

Avoid a detailed answer to this question as far as possible. Be comfortable and confident when answering this question, but stop with one or two lines. Be silent after that. This should avoid this question most of the time. There are very few interviewers who might persist further. If they do, give very general one-line answers unless they ask for a specific incident.

Why This Answer Works

Any elaborate answer to this question is going to make you look too weak to handle stress. Hence, the given answer is brief and it technically answers the question. It doesn't give out any information that can get you rejected. This answer helps skip this question to the maximum extent.

Question 20

Tell me about a time when you had to handle high levels of stress.

Alternative Wording (Variants):

How will you handle this given stressful situation?

Have you ever faced a particularly high-pressure situation at work? Narrate how you handled it.

Give an example of a time when you were confronted with a particularly challenging situation and had to manage your stress levels effectively?

Why They Ask This Question

This is a way different question from the previous one. Here, they definitely want you to recount a past incident. Otherwise, they may give you an imaginary situation themselves and ask you how you'll handle it.

Either way, tell them a convincing story. It's best to think of a few incidents beforehand that cover many types of situations. You can take cues from some of the previous example answers to questions such as how you made a difficult decision or how you handled an argument.

Tips to Answer if They Give an Example Stressful Incident

It's difficult to give a one-size-fits-all answer here. Think of the most pragmatic step for that situation with the company's interest in mind. Say you'll do that. Back up your answer with statistics, facts and other relevant info. If you need more details, ask for it. If they refuse to give more details but still want a decision, be logical in making assumptions that your decision will rely on. Make sure your plan of action is flexible enough to cover all possible cases or outcomes. When you explain your answer, also demonstrate that you'll exercise people skills without using the word "people skills".

Tips to Answer if They Ask for a Stressful Incident from Your Past

All example answers given for "What is your greatest professional achievement?" and tips therein hold good for this question also.

Never Say

Never avoid this question like you did the previous. The interviewer might start with the previous question and then ask for an example incident, which is this question. You want to switch modes quickly and narrate your incident.

When narrating, never talk about your personal feelings. The interviewer doesn't want that. In fact, they want to see that you gave no room for personal feelings in this situation. Saying things like you felt hurt etc. will make you look weak no matter how you say it. Instead, simply mention how the situation got more complicated than you had initially planned and what you did logically (not emotionally).

In your answer, never use words like "stress", "tension", "frustration" etc. even if the question uses these words. You want to demonstrate that while the situation was tough, you never got stressed. This is the whole point of answering this question.

How to Say It

This question is a great opportunity to show how tough you are and the level of difficulties you can handle. So, be confident and state the facts. Focus more about the demands of the work itself and how logically you dealt with it. Make your story easily understandable. Ask a friend or consultant if your example incident sounds good from an interviewer's viewpoint.

Why This Answer Works

This answer works because it focuses more on the challenge part rather than the feelings part. It subtly demonstrates how hardheaded you can be without overtly saying it.

Question 21

How comfortable are you working with ambiguity?

Alternative Wording (Variants):

What is your tolerance for ambiguity?

What will you do when you have to make a decision with unclear or incomplete information?

Tell me about a time when you had to work on a project with vague goals or objectives.

How do you handle situations where there is no definitive answer or solution?

Why They Ask This Question

This is usually a top-management or middle-management interview question. If they ask this question, then the position probably involves dealing with unexpected challenges on a daily basis. These challenges may be difficult even to understand in the first place, let alone solve. The last thing you want to do is give textbook answers to this question.

In these situations, lack of information will be the biggest frustrating factor. You'll need to fill in the gaps with just your critical-thinking skills. You'll mostly have to act alone, take sizable risks but come out successful. This is no easy question by any means, but one that sets the men apart from the boys.

Example Answer

I am very comfortable working with ambiguity. I always feel very satisfied when I have to figure out the details myself. It gives me a lot of thrill and excitement to solve problems that are vague in nature.

For instance, in my previous job, I was the supervisor for a small sub-team. The manager of the team, who is also my boss, suddenly got hospitalized. So, I became the acting manager for the entire team until he got back. The role was quite an increase for me way above my experience level. But we expected no major challenge or incident, and my boss is expected to be back soon. So, I figured I could do this role pretty smoothly.

However, during this time, a key raw material supplier of ours suddenly went out of business. This news came as a shock to me. They can't supply us anymore, which means our daily production will take a major hit. This was an unexpected blow to the company's daily activities. It could potentially create huge losses.

I wasn't given any instructions on how to find a new supplier. Since my manager was in no position to talk, I couldn't contact him. Besides my manager, there was nobody to ask within our company. This responsibility single-handedly fell on me.

I read up as much as possible about the raw materials, raw material standards, the available suppliers nearby, price ranges and online reviews. I even asked the opinions of a few contacts I had in the industry.

After all that massive effort, I found a new supplier inside our town and hired them. We turned the situation around and had a steady stream of raw material supply. Within a week, we brought our production back to full speed. When my manager returned from the hospital, he appreciated my efforts and told me I did the right thing.

Never Say

The first instinct for anybody when asked about ambiguity is discomfort. So, you'll impulsively feel like saying you're not comfortable. However, saying so is the quickest way to get disqualified. Always say you can handle ambiguity.

How to Say It

Make sure to tell a story where you initially lacked crucial information for a task, but later found it out and completed the task. A story without this part isn't going to be convincing.

Why This Answer Works

Confidently saying that you can handle ambiguity is exactly the interviewer wants to hear. Having an incident ready is going to be a huge plus on your part. By narrating the incident in an easy-to-understand way, you're making sure that the interviewer has no room to reject you.

Question 22

How would you describe your own personality?

Alternative Wording (Variants):

Describe yourself in 3 (or more) words.

Why They Ask This Question

Employers want to know what impact your personality type will have on your job i.e., whether your personality type will help or hurt your performance. Likewise, they also want to know whether your personality type will fit with the existing team and company culture. For instance, lazy personalities won't work hard, argumentative people won't be friendly with others and so on.

To answer this question, don't start describing your actual personality type. They're not interested in that. Just describe yourself with personality traits that most employers will find appealing. Extra points if you can add traits from the job requirements list. For instance, if the job requirement asks for attention to detail, you can describe yourself as meticulous.

While you're at it, try to use *more descriptive* words than usual. Employers are often tired of hearing the same words over and over like hardworking, confident, passionate, efficient, competent, honest or creative. There's absolutely nothing wrong with these words as such. They are great words, but since every candidate uses the same words, you want to use less frequent but more meaningful words like industrious, reliable, focused, organized, results driven, accommodating, goal oriented and supportive.

Ideal Answer

I'd describe myself as an industrious, meticulous and reliable person who thrives in an environment of challenge. I believe in being self-motivated and cooperative to the management so that they need not spend much time supervising and guiding me. I can be flexible and accommodating to the changes in the work environment while being consistent at my work. I am motivated by complicated tasks that push me to be meticulous. I always support my coworkers in whichever way possible because we need to succeed as a team ultimately. To me, success means achieving the goals set forward by the management and I will be relentless at achieving it.

Never Say

Definitely don't talk about your personal life and your behavior there. That's none of their concern. Don't talk about any trait that doesn't relate to the job you've applied to.

Needless to say, always mention only positive attributes. Some things while seeming positive on the outset may also be seen as a negative. For instance, ambitious may sound positive in general, but the interviewer might think they'll constantly need to promote you to keep you motivated and this could eliminate you straightaway.

How to Say It

Don't feel stunned by this question. Be happy as you answer it. You're describing yourself after all. Say every word like you mean it. Your tone should be genuine as you describe every trait. You want the interviewer to think you're sincere about what you're saying.

Why This Answer Works

Managers want to get an impression about you as quickly as possible. They also want to know whether you've understood the job requirements. Asking to describe your own personality is a direct way to know that. The given answer lists many personality traits most employers would love to have. Saying it as it is will sound appealing to most interviewers. Obviously, you can modify it, add a few traits that your particular employer is looking for and create a customized answer, which is going to be far more effective. Just make sure you don't sound like every other candidate and actually have something meaningful to say.

Question 23

What do you like to do outside of work?

Alternative Wording (Variants):

What are your interests besides career?

What type of hobbies do you have?

Do you engage in any extracurricular activities?

How do you spend your free time?

Why They Ask This Question

For a relatively inexperienced job seeker, this question might seem innocent. You might be tempted to let your hair down a little and frankly tell them what your real hobbies are. Is this question really meant in a lighthearted tone? Think again.

Your interviewer's only job is to get an idea about you. This idea will help decide whether or not to hire you. Your hobbies are a very good opportunity for them. For instance, answering that you play chess in your free time means you're intelligent and you spend your time sharpening your strategizing skills. Good for management and problem-solving jobs. If you say your hobby is painting, then you're creative – good for designing jobs. Answering that you play soccer means you're engaging in physical exercise, team building, planning and stress handling all in one go. Super good. If you say you attend networking events in your spare time, it means you are a people's person, and presumably, you might have lots of contacts. Great for the corporate world.

If you say you hang out with friends after work, the interviewer might think you're more given to enjoyment than work. This means you may slack at work. If you say you watch TV in your spare time, it comes off as being a couch potato (even if you're not). Saying that household chores or taking care of family gives you no free time, they'll think you're bad at time management. See the point?

I am not saying any of the above conclusions are fair. Of course, everybody loves to hang out with friends and watch TV etc., but your interviewer doesn't want you to say that. The interviewer wants to imagine you doing a professional, productive or skill-building activity even outside of work. You want to answer with this in mind.

Acceptable Answers

While there is no fixed answer to this question, you want to pick one that is seen in a positive light generally and one that might potentially improve your day-to-day work at their company. Some acceptable answers include gym, professional sports, yoga, attending corporate or professional events, event management, soft skills classes and workshops, correspondence courses, reading, gardening, learning or playing music, volunteering etc.

Never Say

Never mention any side activity that doesn't involve a skill. Don't mention an activity that's seen as unproductive (any activity done for entertainment alone is considered unproductive). The interviewer is primarily looking for an activity involving a skill that will directly or indirectly improve your daily work.

Definitely don't say anything that's considered lazy or irresponsible such as TV, movies, video games, dating, drinking, gambling etc. Also, don't show that you have a connection to or interest in a specific religious group, political party or sports team. This could also be something as silly as a Harry Potter fan club or your favorite Pokémon's Facebook group. While it may be tempting to portray your favorite political party's meeting as a networking event, you have no idea what the interviewer's political views are. This could cost you the job.

Finally, don't say you have a side business or speak of any activity that could potentially turn into a side business (such as freelancing). This is because the employer might think you'll leave this job if your side business becomes successful enough to pay your bills.

Why Such an Answer Works

When you follow all the instructions given here, your answer will show that you're productive even in your hobbies. It makes you look like you have goals outside of work. This is a very positive impression and will increase your chances of getting hired.

Question 24

What was the last book you read?

Alternative Wording (Variants):

What was the last movie you saw?
 What was the last sporting event you attended?
What was the last song that you listened to?
What was the last YouTube video you saw?

Why They Ask This Question

This is another way of asking about your hobbies but in a very specific way. There are two ways the interviewer can judge you here – if you mention a movie or sporting event, the interviewer will make an assumption about your personality (psychological assessment, which is okay), or they may think you're too much of a movie buff or sports fan, which is not okay because they'll think it'll hinder your performance. This is also true for a novel or a short story.

Obviously, don't mention the actual last movie you watched or your actual favorite song. Don't say the name of any movie or event that's controversial. Also, don't show yourself to be a fan of any actor, singer, YouTuber, author or sportsperson. You have no idea what kind of bias the interviewer or organization holds.

The best way to answer this kind of question is to tell them that you're not regularly into doing these things. The last movie you saw or sporting event you went to was something that's highly important, successful, exemplary, professional and neutral work in that field. The reason you did it was you believed it'll improve you in some way or give you some knowledge.

After you mention your favorite book, movie or song, spend one or two more sentences on why you chose it and what you learned from it. Mention a line on how it improved your life. It'd help if you've read at least one book or remember at least one movie or song or sporting event. It should be appropriate enough to mention in an interview.

Example Answer 1

I make it a point to read self-help books a lot because I can improve myself as a human being. The last book I read was *How to Win Friends and Influence People* by Dale Carnegie. It was a completely groundbreaking insight into how people behave in different situations. The book clearly states how small changes in our behavior when dealing with others can lead to a huge success in life. It's astounding to think that this book is almost a century old but the principles mentioned in the book are relevant even today. Reading this book has helped me become a better employee at work and improved my people skills a lot. I feel everyone who is serious about succeeding in life should read it at least once.

Example Answer 2

I usually don't watch a lot of movies. I'll watch it only if it's a truly well-made movie, preferably with a good message or a historical depiction. A movie I saw recently was *The Pursuit of Happyness*. The plot, as you may know, is based on the true-life story of motivational speaker Chris Gardner. Gardner struggles as a salesman in the '80s. He invested all his money in his business but it takes a long time for him to earn back everything. He becomes homeless in the meantime. On top of this, his wife leaves him and Gardener becomes a single dad with no one to take care of his young son. The film has been an inspiration for me to work harder in real life and taught me that a healthy amount of confidence can overcome any struggle.

(Pick a movie that has a serious message, that's inspirational and, preferably, one with historical or biographical value. This will make them think you're a professional. Choosing to talk about a purely entertaining movie such as a comedy will make them think you're not serious. Don't mention more than one movie, even when asked, as it may make you look like a movie buff i.e., a potential slacker.)

Never Say

Don't say you've never read a book. It makes you come off as someone not wanting to learn anything new. Don't say you have never watched a movie, listened to a song or attended a sporting event. The interviewer knows it's a lie. Preferably, don't pick a work of entertainment like a fantasy novel or a comedy. Don't talk about songs with swear words or other works with offensive content. For sporting events, pick those that are more professional in nature.

How to Say It

Keep it short. Preferably, go with an option that everybody agrees is a good work. The interviewer will like it if you can tell them an advantageous reason for choosing it, what you liked in it and what you learned from it – even better if what you learned will somehow help you in your work. The interviewer will get an idea about your personality type that way. Be happy as you answer it so that you can show how much you enjoyed learning from it.

Why Such Answers Work

Such answers work because there's nothing negative a sane interviewer can conclude. The answers mention famous works that most people consider inspiring and well made. Picking a self-help book, biographical movie or motivational song helps the interviewer visualize you in a more professional light. Answering it this way is going to make you come off as very positive.

Question 25

What motivates you?

Alternative Wording (Variants):

What are you passionate about?

Why They Ask This Question

This is another way of asking why you want this job. If you're new to giving job interviews, you may misunderstand this question as your general hobbies outside of work. Remember, unless the interviewer specifically mentions outside of work, every question is about work.

The only answer to this question is this job.

Ideal Answer

I am very passionate about this job and this field. What motivates me is the challenge that comes with performing [requirement 1], [requirement 2] and [requirement 3]. While in a similar role in my previous job, the objective was only to [insert ordinary objective here]. However, I was motivated to go above and beyond the call of duty and achieved [achievement 1], [achievement 2] and [achievement 3]. My previous manager and the top management were so happy with my performance. Seeing their satisfied faces was the biggest motivating factor for me.

Never Say

Saying anything like money, perks in the job, promotion, praise, pay raise, entertainment, enjoyment or other material gains is grounds for rejection straightaway. Any answer that implies "I don't know what motivates me" is going to be bad as well. The only acceptable answers are you're motivated by seeing your company succeed, giving your best performance and making your bosses happy.

How to Say It

Show excitement as you talk about the daily work and how much you like doing it. Highlight the benefit they as a company can get from you.

Why This Answer Works

Managers already have a hard time motivating employees. Lack of employee motivation is one of the leading causes of employee turnover. This is like a slow cancer that can spread in the organization. If the interviewer sees that you're already excited and motivated about the work, then you're already a better hire than most others. Your excitement may even be infectious once you get on board. This should come off as a strong reason to hire you.

Question 26

Did you ever think of leaving your present position before? If so, what do you think held you there?

Why They Ask This Question

This is just a fancy way of asking if you left your previous job because it wasn't good enough. Also, TLDR, the answer is no. It's always a no. Answering yes will make you look like an opportunist who'll jump ship when the time is right.

Ideal Answer

My present company has been one of the best employers I've had in my career. The work environment is quite conducive, and my manager and coworkers are a breeze to work with. During my tenure I've had the pleasure to work on a varied set of projects including [project 1], [project 2] and [project 3] and learned a lot in the process. Because of everybody's support, I even achieved [achievement 1], [achievement 2] and [achievement 3]. Leaving my present employer never even crossed my mind before.

(If they follow up with "So, why are you leaving now then?" you can answer it with the same answer for "why are you leaving your current job?")

Never Say

Don't complain about your old employer. Don't say you tried to leave previously but couldn't get a job anywhere else etc. Don't say you stayed back because they offered a pay raise or promotion. Saying any of these things will make your resume fly to the trash in business class.

How to Say It

Be confident in your story. Maintain your story even if they doubt it or ask follow-up questions. Keep it short, and stay silent afterward.

Why This Answer Works

This is a trick question. They want to eliminate you here, and you shouldn't let them. The given answer leaves no room for this. It says a firm no. Further, the given answer praises the previous employer, which is a positive.

Question 27

What did you not like about your last job and why?

Alternative Wording (Variants):

If there is one thing you wish was different in your previous job, what would it be?

If you could give your previous employer a suggestion for improvement, what would it be?

Why They Ask This Question

This is another way of asking the previous question but with a more cunning approach. Same rules as the previous question. The answer is always nothing.

Ideal Answer

I loved working for my last employer. The work culture was great and I had a very fostering relationship with everybody there. The management was very supportive. They included me in training sessions, meetings, research programs, and even asked my professional opinion on important matters. Because of their support, I achieved [achievement 1], [achievement 2] and [achievement 3]. I can honestly tell you that I've grown a lot as a person because of my previous organization. There's not a single thing I'd change.

Never Say

Never say you would change something unless you want to bid adieu to this job opening.

How to Say It

Say it like you mean it. Maintain your story even if they doubt it or ask follow-up questions. Smile as you answer this question. Keep it short, and stay silent afterward.

Why This Answer Works

The interviewer wants to get the dirt on you here. They want to know if you will, in any way, complain about your previous employer. Even if they word it as a suggestion and you meant it as a suggestion, it's going to be seen as a complaint anyway. So, the best thing to say is "I'd change nothing" and this answer does precisely that. Just saying nothing without any explanation is going to stir up more questions or doubts. So, you best praise your previous employer before saying you'd change nothing. That's exactly what the given answer does.

Question 28

Why have you not achieved a better position given your age and experience?

Alternative Wording (Variants):

Why are you not a [insert higher position here] yet?
Given your experience and achievements, don't you think you have been underemployed?

Why They Ask This Question

This is both a trap question and a confidence tester. This time, they have nitpicked something specific. They want to know if you feel like an underachiever. If you do, then you'll want a promotion in this job as soon as possible. As we have seen already, they don't want candidates who aim for a higher position. They want only those candidates who are happy with this position for the foreseeable future.

If they ask this question in a tone that's especially condescending or demeaning, it may be a stress interview. You want to seriously consider leaving the interview. Same goes for if they don't accept your answer and start digging too much into this. This is because chances are that the company culture and daily work environment is going to be this condescending and insulting. If they ask this in a more matter-of-fact tone, you may consider giving a genuine response.

In case you decide to stay back and answer, here is what you need to know: if you tried to give an answer to this directly, you risk saying something bad about your previous employer. You can't beat around the bush too much either as the interviewer might see through your pretense. The answer has to be balanced.

Ideal Answer

That's a great question. I began my career as a [insert starting position here]. After gaining [number] of years of experience, I was promoted to [next position name]. A few years into that role, I was made [next position name] and finally got the role of [current position]. I believe that career progression isn't solely based on age and experience, but also on a combination of factors including opportunities, competition and probability. I've been getting promoted periodically based on what each management thought fit and viable at the time. And I am very grateful to the management. In my current role, I have been consistently excelling as you can see from my resume. I enjoy my work. As the [current position], I have achieved [achievement 1], [achievement 2] and [achievement 3]. While I'll continue to put in my best at work, I believe promotions are something for the management to decide. I'll be happy with any decision the management makes.

Never Say

As soon as this question is asked, don't show anger, disappointment, frustration, sadness, lack of confidence or any other negative emotion. You can surely take a moment to think, but have a neutral or positive expression as you do.

Don't blame anybody or anything else in your answer. This is the worst way to fail this question. Realize that not achieving a higher position isn't a fault in the first place. There's no set rule that anybody who has reached a certain age or experience level has to be in a certain position. You have no explaining to do to anybody. So, don't go into justification mode. You're answering this question not because you have to justify but because you want to win this interview.

If you feel insulted by this question, that's normal. However, don't shout at, berate, condescend back at or mock the interviewer. All this is going to bear negatively on you and might even affect your future chances at other companies. You have no idea who's connected to whom. If you feel too uncomfortable or feel this isn't working out, just walk out.

How to Say It

Be happy and willing to answer this question. Matter of fact, keep smiling. Say what you have to with confidence, and then stop talking. The interviewer might wear an unimpressed expression, create an awkward silence situation or give an uneasy look. If you feel you have answered the question, stay silent. Don't feel the need to fill any awkward silences with more talk. This will make you look diffident or desperate.

Why This Answer Works

The best you can do for this question is to mention your past promotions and then take the focus away from you. Explain that there are so many more factors involved. The given answer does all this while also explaining that you're constantly putting in effort. It also leaves the final decision to the management, showing obedience and respect. To any fair interviewer, this answer will be quite convincing.

Question 29

Personal questions about relationship status, children, own house, parents, religion, age, ethnicity etc.

Why They Ask This Question

Believe it or not, some interviewers can be unprofessional, even in well-known, well-established organizations. These are intrusive busybodies who enjoy poking their noses into others' business. They love to stereotype or judge every interviewee. They usually have it written all over their face.

If they ask any impertinent or personal question, it's best to directly say so. Add that you're willing to discuss only things related to this job. If this behavior continues, storm out of the room and see if you can report this behavior to HR or other relevant department. In case there's no such viable option, you can check if they broke any laws. Depending on where you live, it may be illegal to ask some of these questions. You can report them to law enforcement, if appropriate.

If the question wasn't illegal as such, but uncalled-for for the given situation, you still want to evaluate whether or not to continue the interview. If you accept the intrusiveness now, chances are the entire company culture is going to be this way. If they don't respect boundaries and treat you respectfully during the interview, fat chance they'll do so later on.

If this happened to you, I'd urge you to post about it on employer review sites. There are many sites that let you post anonymously. Your post might save hundreds of interviewees the trouble.

Possible Answers

- Can you help me understand in what way this question is related to this job?
- I'd appreciate it if you can keep this discussion professional and pertinent to this job.
- I prefer not to discuss personal matters that are unrelated to the job.
- I want to focus only on discussing my suitability for this position.
- If I hear one more impertinent question from you, I'll have to report you.

Never Say

Even in this situation, I'd urge you to keep calm. Don't use swear words, call the interviewer names or shout at them. These things might be twisted back on you later on. Just evaluate whether to respond, report or leave.

How to Say It

Say it in a firm tone. Show that you're not the one to take such behavior lightly.

<u>Why These Answers Work</u>

The given responses set the right boundaries and put the interviewer in line. In case they don't work, you can still communicate your intolerance by reporting or leaving.

Question 30

How important is money to you?

Alternative Wording (Variants):

To what degree do you value money?

How much does money matter to you?

How significant is money in a person's life?

Why They Ask This Question

They want to know if you're after this job only for the money. While everybody knows most people are only after the salary, maybe even the interviewer themselves is only after the salary, we are still required to play this fake game.

The best way to answer this is to say that money is necessary to fulfill basic needs but there are also other priorities in life. Explain that while money is very much important to you to meet your necessities, it's not the reason you chose this job. Mention reasons like personal interest in work, skill set, company culture, strong leadership, good reputation, quality training, opportunities for self-improvement, fair treatment, challenging environment, interesting projects and so on.

Ideal Answer

Money is important to me because it gives me financial stability and a means to support myself and my family. Money's importance can never be understated. However, it's not the sole driving factor in my career decisions. I am more focused on finding a role that aligns with my skill set, where I can contribute meaningfully and make a positive impact. To me, success is achieving the goals set forward by my organization and finding fulfillment in the process of doing so. Money is simply a means and not the end.

Never Say

Obviously, never say all you care about is money. Also, never say money is not important to you. Saying either of these will fail you instantly. Make sure your answer is balanced between these two. If you feel uncomfortable, don't show it. Don't be frustrated if they ask follow-up questions.

How to Say It

Practice saying the given answer multiple times at home in front of a mirror. Practice until the answer comes naturally to you in your interview. Be confident as you say it and avoid the feeling of needing to overexplain this answer.

Why This Answer Works

This answer works because it doesn't take any extreme stance. The answer emphasizes the importance of money as well as other factors that go into making any career decision. It clarifies that money is only one of the many factors involved. In most cases, this balanced approach is going to be convincing to most interviewers.

Question 31

Will you be out to take your boss's job?

Alternative Wording (Variants):

If you could have any position in this organization, which one would you choose?

How important is progressing to higher positions to you?

Don't you think you're overqualified for this position?

Will you feel underemployed in this position?

Is there a better position in this organization that you would rather be offered?

Why They Ask This Question

This question is very similar to "Where do you see yourself in 5 years?" and its variants. The difference is this one is more direct. Here, the question isn't about whether you want to go up the ladder but when and how. While the answer is going to be the same mostly, the way in which you say it should be subtly altered.

Ideal Answer

Career progression is very important for everybody. If the organization offers a higher position, nobody would pass it up. I am no exception. However, at the present stage in my career, I want to get into this position. I feel my current skill set and experience can be put to best use as a [name of the position applied for]. In this role, I hope to become a high-performing and productive employee who can be counted upon to be consistent and finish tasks within time. I am open to taking up a better position only if the organization sees me fit and feels it's time. I am not the sort of person to take someone else's job.

Never Say

Obviously, never say you'll take your boss's job. Also, never say or hint that you want a higher position. You want to show you're more focused on this role you've applied for.

How to Say It

This question may be a test, an elimination game or a genuine fear the interviewer has. In any case, assure them that you'll not want any other position besides this one. Talk more about how you'll contribute in this role. This will show that you've put in enough thought about staying this position.

Why This Answer Works

This answer will ease any worries the interviewer might have about you. It handles a brutally straightforward question smoothly such that the interviewer will gain confidence in you, preferably over other applicants.

Question 32

If I spoke with your current (or former) boss, what would he or she say your greatest strengths and weaknesses are?

Why They Ask This Question

There are two parts to this question – your strengths and weaknesses, your relationship with your boss. The interviewer wants to know both of these through this single question. The interviewer is also going to note if this question makes you uncomfortable.

You want to boldly highlight your strengths for this question no matter whether your boss would actually say them. In most cases, the interviewer isn't going to call up and ask your boss. This question is meant as a confidence tester.

Ideally, portray any three job requirements as your strengths. For weaknesses, talk about only one weakness unrelated to this job that's not really a weakness. While you do this, also demonstrate that you had a great relationship with your boss. You can take cues from previous answers.

Ideal Answer

Oh, I was fortunate enough to have a very understanding and easy-to-work-with boss in my previous job. She'd often appreciate me and guide me on improving my work. I feel very grateful toward her. Under her leadership, I performed [related job activity 1], [related job activity 2] and [related job activity 3], which gave me a lot of experience.

If you happened to ask my previous boss about my strengths, I reckon she'd say my biggest strengths are [job requirement 1], [job requirement 2] and [job requirement 3].

While I was very good at doing [insert strength here], my boss also noted that I was not doing [insert weakness here] effectively. I was doing [insert mistake here] while I am supposed to do [insert how it should be done here]. She suggested that I do [insert suggestion from boss here] so that I can prevent or offset what I was doing wrong. After I implemented her suggestion, I have never had that problem again.

Never Say

Never say you don't know what your boss will say. Never say your boss has never given any feedback to you. Every boss would've given at least one small suggestion or appreciation. Never ever talk bad about your boss. Don't say you have no idea what your weakness is. You should put in some forethought and come up with a weakness that's not really a weakness and something that can be easily solved.

How to Say It

Feel happy that you were asked this question. This question is a great opportunity to demonstrate both your good relationship with your boss as well as your strengths and weaknesses. Have your points prepared well in advance so that they are on the top of your mind. Practice saying the given answer multiple times at home, in front of a mirror, so that it becomes natural when you say it in your interview. Keep it short and simple.

Why This Answer Works

This answer works because it begins with praising and being thankful about your previous boss. It also implies that you had a supportive boss. This in turn might give the impression that your previous boss won't say anything negative about you. Exactly what the interviewer wants to know.

Question 33

Do you prefer line work or staff work?

What Is Line Work and Staff Work?

Line work (not to be confused with line of work) or line function is any work that directly contributes to the core work of the organization. For instance, in a car factory, the core work is assembling cars – the assembly line workers and all their managers are the line workers. The line workers form the company's command hierarchy, including all levels of management. When line workers don't work, the organization's output (quantity) is directly affected.

Staff work or staff function (not to be confused with members of staff) is any work that's not directly part of the core work but performs a support function that helps the core work operate smoothly (quality). For instance, human resources, accounting, IT, marketing, public relations, legal team etc. form the support teams in an organization. While an organization can theoretically carry on without support functions, a weak support team will indirectly affect the organization's work pace, communication, coordination, employee retention, customer retention, cost efficiency, time efficiency and public image.

Furthermore, whether a position is line or staff depends also on what the company does. If you're an accountant, but you join an IT company, you'll be a staff team member.

If you join an accounting firm, you'll be a line team member.

Why They Ask This Question

The reason they ask this is twofold. First, the interviewer wants to know if you understand the difference between line and staff work. You must know where your position fits in this context. Hiring managers hate employees who just want to mindlessly do their work and get away with it. Everybody's work fits into the big picture like a jigsaw puzzle. Managers want you to understand exactly which jigsaw piece you're working on. They also want you to know that the jigsaw piece can change shape or size depending on the changing environment, client requirements, practical problems etc.

If you're placed in the line team, but you don't perform as expected, they'll instantly face the consequences. The output of the organization will be directly affected. On the other hand, if you slack in the staff team, there may be no immediate effect but the company's long-term welfare might be in trouble.

The second reason they ask this question is to check if you're serious about this job. If you had applied for a line work position but you answered staff work in the interview, then you're not serious.

Thus, the best answer to this question is to assure the interviewer that you fully understand everything. You should clearly identify the position as line or staff and explain how it fits into the organization. At the same time, also talk about the job responsibilities and how you'll fulfill them.

Ideal Answer (for Line Work Position)

My skill set and area of expertise fit well with a line work position. As you can see from my resume, all my previous positions have been line functions. This position is also line. I totally understand how important this role is for this company. Tasks like [job responsibility 1] and [job responsibility 2] can directly affect the organization's overall output. It's a highly responsible position. I can assure you that I can reliably perform this job to a high standard and within the set amount of time.

(Definitely modify this answer as you need)

Ideal Answer (for Staff Work Position)

This position is a staff function. As you can see from my work history, all my previous positions have been staff work. I totally understand how crucial support functions are for an organization to operate smoothly. In this position, I understand I'll be responsible for [job responsibility 1], [job responsibility 2] and [job responsibility 3]. These functions require [job requirement 1], [job requirement 2] and [job requirement 3] so that they are fulfilled to a high standard. Given my work experience and qualifications, I am fully prepared to hit the ground running and exceed expectations in this role.

(Definitely modify this answer as you need)

<u>Never Say</u>

Don't ask what line functions and staff functions are back to the interviewer. While it's understandable that some job seekers (esp. recent graduates) may not know these things, interviewers expect you to know them at least at a basic level. Not knowing this can make you seem unfit for any job.

<u>How to Say It</u>

Say it like you've always wanted to work in line or staff position, even if it's not the case. It's best if your past experience aligns with it. Through your tone of voice, genuinely assure the interviewer.

<u>Why This Answer Works</u>

Answering this question relies on whether you can clearly identify the position as line or staff. Once you have identified, you can confidently use the given answer because it touches upon the importance of line and staff work, explains the job requirements, and ends with assuring the interviewer.

Question 34

What's your opinion on such-and-such sports, political, religious or social event or issue?

Alternative wording (variants):

What's your perspective on [blank] current affair?

Why They Ask This Question

There are two things this question could be intended for – either they want to see if you're following current news and if you can talk about a given topic, or they want to reject you based on any bias you show about this issue.

Believe it or not, there can be interviewers who want to get the dirt on you by smearing you with a label based on whom you support or where your bias is. Based on what you answer, you may be termed racist, bigoted, unintelligent, politically motivated etc. Such sensitive and potentially dangerous topics should never be discussed in the workplace and certainly not in an interview. If you feel the interviewer is asking you something they shouldn't be (which is quite likely), it's best to directly but politely tell them.

You also want to evaluate if you should continue the interview at all – this organization could have more such people asking impertinent questions all the time. In such places, opportunities like promotion may not be on merit. Discrimination and favoritism may be an open secret. If you joined this organization, people may hate you or take offense at you about everything for no real reason. They'll most probably treat you badly and deny you opportunities.

On the off chance that they do ask you this question genuinely, you can go forward and answer it in a neutral tone, weighing the pros and cons equally and ultimately stating how it'll benefit or affect the organization. While answering, refrain from taking any side. If you must choose a side, don't come off as too strong in doing so. Instead, state your position humbly and base it on ample evidence.

Example Replies to Avoid the Question (if It's Irrelevant/Inappropriate)

- Can you help me understand in what way this question is related to this job?
- I'd appreciate it if you can keep this discussion pertinent to this job.
- I prefer not to discuss other matters that are unrelated to the job.
- I want to focus on discussing my suitability for this position.
- I believe in keeping such discussions off the workplace.

Example Answer if the Question Is Genuine (for a Financial Analyst Position)

Q: What do you think of the tax policies in the recent federal budget?

A: This year, the government has decided to decrease tax rates for various businesses. Some of these businesses could be this company's clients. Since this is a financial firm that offers investment consultation, many clients will be consulting here about where to invest the new tax savings. This means more business for this company this year.

(In this case, the interviewer wanted to know if the candidate was quick enough to associate the federal budget with the company's business. Note that the given answer directly makes the connection without touching on anything sensitive or unnecessary. No personal opinion, praise or criticism on the matter as news outlets may do – just how it's relevant. The given answer also demonstrates keen understanding of the financial firm's business, what the clients want and why the interviewer is asking this question. Deciding whether a current issue question is relevant is always based on context.)

Never Say

Don't be rude to the interviewer even if the question is irrelevant. Maybe there's some relevance that you haven't thought of. Give them the benefit of doubt. Even if it turns out to be irrelevant after all, still be polite.

How to Say It

Whether you decide to answer or avoid, be confident. If you choose to answer, be ready with the facts and figures to support your answer.

Why This Technique Works

This technique works because first it identifies the relevance of the current affair or issue. This step is crucial. Once the relevance is clear, this technique explains how it'll affect the organization, which is what employers expect. In addition, this technique also avoids bias or judgment.

Question 35

If you were an, which one would you be?

Alternative Wording (Variants):

If you could be any bird, which bird would you be?
If you could be any insect, which one would you be?
If you were an ice cream flavor, what would it be?
If you could be a tree, which tree would you choose?

Why They Ask This Question

This a famous psychological assessment question. To those relatively new to giving job interviews, this might seem odd. If it did, don't give the interviewer a "What the heck are you asking?" kind of look. The interviewer asks this question because they want to know your psychology. If you choose dog as your animal, you're loyal and obedient. If you choose eagle as your bird, then you may be seen as high-flying and predatory. If you choose vanilla as your ice cream, you come plain without any extras. You get the idea.

If you think this is a terrible way of judging candidates, I am totally with you. However, they use this as an elimination game mostly.

To best answer this question, consider the position you're applying for and the job requirements listed. Choose an animal or bird that aligns with those requirements. Think whether the position is that of a leader or a follower. Do you need to work with machines or human beings? Does this position involve taking risks or playing it safe? Do you need to be detail-oriented or focus only on the big picture? Do you need to bring in variety or consistency? Such questions will help you choose an animal or bird that's relevant.

The most important part is to explain why you chose that thing. The reason you mention should directly fulfill a requirement for this job position.

Example Answer 1 (Animal, for a Manager's Position)

I'd be a lion. Lions are good leaders, brave in their approach. They choose their targets only after making sure they can definitely chase them down. They lock their vision on to their target and tenaciously run after them without giving up. Just like a lion, I'd love to bring tangible results to my employer.

Example Answer 2 (Insect, for a Follower's Position)

I'd prefer to be a bee. Bees are known for their hard work and consistency. They are team players with perfect coordination. They communicate well with each other. Bees have a strong division of labor. Every bee has its own duty, which it does without being told. Bees as a team make it a point to serve and safeguard the queen, who is their leader, and raise the young ones until they have reached maturity. In the end, they produce a sweet result, which pays off for all their hard work.

Example Answer 3 (Ice Cream, for an Entry-Level Position)

I'd choose to be mint chocolate chip because I am refreshing. I bring a burst of energy to any team or project I am involved in.

Example Answer 4 (Bird)

If I had to choose a bird, I suppose I'd be a penguin. Penguins have incredible resilience and adaptability to challenging environments. Penguins also have a strong sense of community and help each other out when there is a need. The males and females work as a team to reach their goal which is to raise young ones.

Never Say

Don't say you don't know which animal or bird to choose. It's best to think of something beforehand, failing which, something convincing on the spot. Don't say you don't know why you chose that animal or bird. You have to give a strong reason for choosing it. It's better to say something instead of nothing. Some interviewers may appreciate trying. If you don't like this question, don't mock the interviewer or give a negative look. This could reject you.

How to Say It

Say it confidently. Keep it short. Keep the explanation simple and straightforward. No need to try too hard or over explain your choice.

<u>Why These Answers Work</u>

These answers work because they understand the psychology behind this question. Then, they proceed with a choice of animal or bird relative to the position applied for, which is important. Finally, the answers also explain the rationale behind the choice so that it makes a positive impression as you end it.

Question 36

If you could have dinner with any fictional character, who would it be and why?

Alternative Wording (Variants):

If you could have dinner with any famous person, who would it be and why?

Why They Ask This Question

This is very similar to the previous question, but not the same. While the interviewer assessed your personality type with the previous question, here they want to understand the type of person you like and would accommodate well with. Then they'll decide your fit with the existing team members.

When choosing a fictional character, you want to pick one that's seen under a more serious light. Preferably, the character has to be logical, practical and good at some specific work. Bonus points if the character's positives align with the requirements of the current position.

Example Answer 1

If I could have dinner with any fictional character, I'd choose Sherlock Holmes. I've always admired how he analyzes situations in ways most people don't usually think of. He solves intricate problems quickly like they were obvious. He uses the right mix of social skills and logical reasoning to simplify the problem down to its basic variables. This is something I have always wanted to learn from somebody like him.

Example Answer 2

I'd appreciate it if I can have dinner with Mr. Bill Gates. His company's line of operating systems, Windows, is the most widely used in the PC market. It's astounding that even after 40+ years of Windows' inception, it still dominates the industry. Windows was what made computers accessible to literally everyone. You need not be a technical person but still use Windows. At the time of launch, Windows was cheaper than the alternatives, so everyone opted for it. Windows was also partly responsible for standardizing the PC hardware market. All in all, Mr. Bill Gates revolutionized the PC market with Windows. I'd love to learn from him how he created a product that has stayed at the top of the market for decades.

Example Answer 3

I'd choose Hermione Granger from the *Harry Potter* series. Hermione has always inspired me with her intelligence, bravery and excellence at what she does. She's the most studious character in the series with a lot of knowledge on various subjects. She always keeps herself busy and has never had a problem with time management. I'd love to learn how she does everything so effortlessly.

Never Say

Don't say you don't know whom to choose. This will make you come off as indecisive. Don't choose a character or person that's less famous. Don't choose the villain in a story or someone who is evil or violent. If a character is vile, no amount of justification can make it look good. Also, don't choose any person or character that's seen as irresponsible or less serious.

How to Say It

Keep it short. Choose a character or person that's well known. Make sure that the interviewer would've likely heard of your character. The reason you chose that character or person should be appropriate for a workplace setting. Keep the explanation simple.

Why These Answers Work

The given answers have all chosen a famous person or character that has admirable qualities any employer would want in their employees. The answers also highlight these qualities using the correct words and examples.

Question 37

How many tennis balls can you fit into a limousine?

Alternative Wording (Variants):

How many basketballs can you fit into an airplane?

Why They Ask This Question

Again, for the uninitiated, this may sound like an odd question to ask in an interview. The interviewers have their reasons though. They are not checking if you know the correct answer. In fact, they don't care about the correct answer. They just want to know how you approach the question before answering it.

Management problems usually come in ambiguous, unintelligible, irregular, abstract and random forms. They don't want you to get intimidated or turned off in such situations. Most managers are tasked with solving problems they don't fully understand. The interviewer will check your immediate reaction to this question. They'll note if you enthusiastically pick up your wits to solve it.

Example Answer 1 (Tennis Balls in Limo)

To begin with, I'll find out the dimensions of a standard tennis ball and calculate the volume using the formula for volume of a sphere. Then, I'll see if the limo's volume is already given in the manufacturer's website, or if they can share this information over e-mail. If not, I'll calculate the volume myself by considering the shape of the limo as one frustum sitting on top of another using the appropriate mathematical formulas.

At first, it'd be easier to calculate the volume if we removed all the seats, steering wheel and other objects. In case those objects need to be inside the limo in our finished work, we can adjust for them later on.

When fitting the balls inside the car, there'll be a lot of space in between the balls. Then, when one layer sits on top of another, the balls are not going to align. We'll need to adjust for these things during our calculation.

Overall, I'd approach this question by breaking it down into easier parts and use logical reasoning to make an estimate.

Example Answer 2 (Basketballs in Airplane)

I would start by calculating the basketball's volume with the formula for the volume of a sphere. Then, I'll find out the total volume of the airplane by checking that model's specifications on the manufacturer's website. I can also e-mail them for it. If this doesn't work, I'll have to make a rough calculation myself. For this, I'll assume the plane is a cylinder and the front and back portions are cones. I'll then use mathematical formulas to calculate the volume of the plane.

Then, I can make my first estimate of the number of balls by simple division. Once we have this estimate, I can start adjusting for the volume left out between the balls and how one layer of balls stacks on top of another etc.

This answer makes a lot of assumptions including that the basketballs are inflated, the seats and other items inside an airplane are removed and only the outer shell of the plane remains.

If the balls are not inflated, then we must find out the least amount of space a deflated basketball will take up. Use that as our basketball's volume. If the seats or other objects need to be placed inside the airplane, we have to subtract their individual volumes from our answer.

In conclusion, I prefer to approach this question logically, mathematically and based on whatever information we can find out. I'll ask the right questions along the way and take into account all possibilities before making my final estimate.

Never Say

Don't get thrown aback by this question or give a confused expression. Don't say you don't know or it's very difficult. The interviewer knows it's a complex problem. They only want to know how you'll handle it. There's no one correct answer here. As long as your approach is logically convincing, you can be as creative as you want. Give enough details to show that you're meticulous in your approach, but not too many details that the interviewer loses patience. Don't take too much time to think.

How to Say It

Be confident in how you'll tackle this problem. Your approach need not be perfect. The interviewer only wants to see how quickly and confidently you come up with a solution. They won't care about the quality of the solution itself. Be mindful of the assumptions you make along the way and mention your assumptions openly. This will make you look more open minded and practical.

Why These Answers Work

These answers work because they clearly explain each step taken in solving the given problem. This gives the interviewer a sense of how you think and how you approach problems in general. The given answers also take into account all the assumptions and practical considerations that are part of the problem.

Question 38

How would you explain the concept of color to someone who was born blind?

Alternative Wording (Variants):

How would you explain the concept of music to someone who was born deaf?

Why They Ask This Question

This is very similar to the previous question. They want you to come up with an approach to tackle a problem. The difference is this problem is much more subjective. In the previous case, everybody understands what balls, limos and airplanes are. On the contrary, in this case, you're explaining visual differences to someone who has no idea what vision is, let alone colors. This question tests your communication skills to its limits.

If you just heard this question for the first time, you could be puzzled. Don't worry. This *is* a tough question! If it makes it any easier, think of this as explaining something technical to someone (like a client or a manager) who isn't a technical person. Thus, you'll have to use as many nontechnical words as possible to convey the basic idea. There's no way anybody is going to do a perfect job here. You just have to try your best. It will help if you can use examples that are easy to imagine or connect to.

<u>Example Answer 1 (Explaining Color to Someone Born Blind)</u>

A completely blind person has no idea of the concept of vision. So, it's better to start with an analogy using other senses.

I'd start with explaining that just like how different things make different sounds, different things have different colors. Colors are variances in vision just like how sounds are variances in hearing. Colors help us tell things apart. Just as sounds can be pleasant or unpleasant, colors can also be pleasing or displeasing when arranged in a certain order.

Based on the color, you can identify common objects. For instance, blood is red, bananas are yellow, snow is white, sky is blue, grass is green and the night is black. Some things are always one color, while others can come in different colors while having the same function. For example, balloons, confetti or clothing may come in different colors but do the same thing. Certain things can also be multicolored such as birds.

Colors can have some common generalized meanings associated with them but this is not a hard-and-fast rule. For instance, the color red is often associated with spicy food and is used in the marketing of chili-flavor snacks. However, fruits like strawberries and cherries are also red, which are exceptions.

Sometimes, things of different nature can also have the same color. For instance, sugar and salt are both white, the fruit orange and pumpkin can both be orange, and bananas and school buses can both be yellow and so on. Even sighted people can get confused between things of the same color and shape. For instance, powdered sugar is going to look exactly like flour unless you smell or taste it.

There are also certain things that you can see completely through such as glass or clear water. Such things are called transparent or colorless.

This is a very basic and oversimplified explanation of what color is. There's definitely a lot more to this, but I hope this will be a good starting point for a blind person.

Example Answer 2 (Explaining Music to Someone Born Deaf)

For this explanation, I am going to assume that the person is completely and irreparably deaf. Sound as a concept is foreign to them. In this case, it's best to explain sound first and then music.

I'd begin with saying that sound is a type of vibration that you sense with your ear just like how you sense vibrations through touch. When your ear senses that vibration, it's called hearing, and what you hear is called a sound. Different objects have different sounds. Based on the sound, you can identify what's making that sound – a bell clanging, a bird chirping, a whistle blowing, a person talking or a train honking.

Some of these sounds can be pleasing to the ear and some of them can be unbearable, just like how some foods taste sweet and others bitter. When something is loud and displeasing it's called noise. Nobody likes them.

Some sounds that come out of an instrument or out of a trained singer's mouth can be pleasing to the ear. This is very similar to how certain colors when put together form beautiful designs or patterns. Such pleasing sounds are called music. They are assembled by musicians in a rhythmic and harmonious way. People often listen to music to relax and feel good. It's also used as therapy in some situations.

While the basic intention of music is to please, it can also be used to set any type of mood. For instance, in movies and TV shows music is used to set the mood for a given situation such as happy, sad, frightening, anxious, angry or anticipating.

Music is an art form that has so many concepts to learn and it takes a lifetime of devotion. People study music in institutes, practice thousands of times and become instrument players, singers and composers. Music is also a highly profitable industry. The recordings of the best musical performances can be worth billions of dollars.

While it's difficult to cover all aspects of music in one explanation, this should be enough for a deaf person to get a rudimentary understanding.

Never Say

Don't be startled or put back by these types of questions. Don't get frustrated or blanked out by them. Do your best to explain whatever you can. Don't overexplain or get into too many details. Just explain what is needed. Focus more on the overall picture rather than specific points.

How To Say It

Always think from the viewpoint of the intended listener and structure your explanation accordingly. Always stick to analogies and examples they'll understand and find easy to connect with. Make your explanation objective and use facts where possible. You're trying to explain a technical subject to a nontechnical person, so don't feel the need to explain everything. Make sure they get the overall picture. Keep the explanation simple while still highlighting some fine details and exceptions.

Why These Answers Work

These answers work because they try to be objective and rational. Since we are explaining something that the listener has no way to experience, the only way to do it is to stick to facts. Thus, these answers focus more on the concrete parts of the concept rather than abstract. They use a cause-and-effect pattern to explain. This way, we can

get the listener up to speed quickly with what they need to
know.

187

Question 39

If you found a wallet on the street with a lot of money inside, what would you do?

Why They Ask This Question

This is a question intended to test your honesty. The answer is always to return it to the owner or hand it over to the police. Even if the interviewer mocks you for being too naïve or gullible, stick to being honest.

Ideal Answer

Well, I'd prefer to return it to the owner. If I saw the owner drop it, I'd inform them. If I found the wallet without the owner and if the street is relatively safe, I'd inspect it to see if there's some information about the owner. If there is, I'd try to contact them. If there's no information, I'll go to the nearest police station and hand the wallet over. If I suspect that the wallet on the street might be dangerous to even touch, then I'll call 911 on the spot.

Never Say

Obviously, never say you'll keep the money. Never seem unsure when saying this answer. Be confident even if the interviewer doesn't seem very impressed. Be 100% sure about being honest no matter what.

How to Say It

Keep it short. Keep it simple. Be direct.

Why This Answer Works

This answer demonstrates honesty from your side. Every employer wants their employees to be honest. Thus, rest assured that this answer is going to easily pass you for this question.

Question 40

What is your management style?

Alternative Wording (Variants):

What is your leadership style?

How do you typically go about managing employees?

What Is Management Style?

In management theory, there are four major management styles (aka leadership styles) – autocratic, stringent, democratic and laissez-faire.

Autocratic is when the manager takes all-powerful, unquestionable authority, allows no employee freedom and puts pressure to get things done.

Democratic is the stark opposite of autocratic. It's where the manager treats everyone equally, delegates tasks within each person's limits and takes a more people-oriented approach.

Stringent is in between autocratic and democratic. A stringent manager has a high level of authority but isn't all-powerful or unquestionable. Work standards will be high but not backbreaking.

Laissez-faire is a management style where the manager doesn't interfere with the employees' work at all. The employees are usually responsible enough to finish the work by themselves.

Why They Ask This Question

They ask this question to know whether your management style will fit with that of this company. In a perfect world, you would answer this question with the same style as what the company follows and you'd be hired. Practically speaking, however, there is no one style that any company follows. Every team inside the company might have its own management style. Every manager within each team might have their own style. In fact, we all have different percentages of each management style within us.

Thus, you can't guess what the interviewer thinks is the right answer. Don't answer this question with a single style. Instead say that you'll adopt each of the aforementioned styles depending on the situation and whom you're managing.

Ideal Answer

The management style I'll adopt depends on many factors including the type of subordinates and the goals we are trying to achieve. If the subordinates are self-starters and are already achieving their goals, it's best to follow a laissez-faire policy. I'll keep my intervention to a minimum. On the other hand, if they slack and have no intention of working hard, it's best to be autocratic or stringent. In a team where there should be a balance of supervision and autonomy, democratic management style is best. Thus, it really depends on a lot of things. I believe a good manager is one who can juggle all styles of management seamlessly depending on the situation.

Never Say

Don't say you'll follow only a single style of management. Don't say you have no idea. Don't sound unsure. Don't overexplain anything.

How to Say It

Keep it short. Show that you're open to adopting any management style they want you to. From any follow-up questions, you can understand what they expect. Once you know that, you can answer accordingly.

Why This Answer Works

The interviewer might reject you if you answered with the wrong management style. This answer clarifies that you're open to all styles of management. The interviewer can't reject you for such an answer.

Question 41

How would you like to be managed?

Alternative Wording (Variants):

How would you prefer your manager dealt with you?

Why They Ask This Question

There are two reasons they may ask this question – either this is another way of asking what's your management style (previous question), or this could be to find out which manager is suitable for you. Anyway, the answer is always either "it depends on the manager" or "in accordance with the company's or team's management style". Any other answer might be grounds for rejection.

Ideal Answer

When it comes to managing me, I'd prefer to be managed in a way that's best for the company. I believe that every company or team cultivates a certain management style for a reason. It's best to adapt to it. Also, every manager might have their own style, and I respect that. How I should be managed is something for the company and the management to decide. I believe in being compliant with what the management decides.

Never Say

Never say you prefer to be managed in a particular way. If your preferred way doesn't suit the company or team, you'll be rejected. The more particular things you mention, the greater your chance of rejection. Show yourself to be open to any style.

How to Say It

Keep it short. Say what you have to say and then stop talking. Wait for the interviewer to move on to the next question. If they insist on a more specific answer, repeat points from the given answer in different words, but ultimately remain open to any style of management.

Why This Answer Works

This answer works because it directly tells them you're open to being managed as per the company's management style. Since this is precisely what the interviewer wants to know, this is the best answer that can be given.

Question 42

What is your working style?

Alternative Wording (Variants):

How would you describe your work style?

Why They Ask This Question

The interviewer wants your work style to align with the work style they expect. Your best bet is to once again stick to the job posting and job requirements list. Mention the things in it as your working style.

Ideal Answer

When it comes to my working style, I am someone who does [job requirement 1], [job requirement 2] and [job requirement 3] while starting the work. During the work, I make sure I do [job skill 1], [job skill 2] and [job skill 3] so that the work is done the best way. I also do [job skill 4] and [job skill 5] to ensure my work is high quality and finishes within time.

(Of course, modify the above answer to your particular situation.)

Never Say

Don't digress from the job requirements. The interviewer isn't interested in knowing your actual working style. They simply want to know whether your style will fit this role's expectations. Your job is to convince them it will.

How to Say It

Make sure every word you say is relevant to this job posting. Your style of working, as you describe it, should accurately paint the ideal employee they have in mind. Make your description as visual as possible so that they can easily imagine you performing in the role. This will make you look like the most suitable candidate among others. If possible, paraphrase the job requirements and skill set.

Why This Answer Works

The given answer directly responds to the question by mentioning the job requirements straight out of the job posting. This easily makes you look like the right fit for the job rather than answering it any other way.

Question 43

How do you prioritize your work?

Alternative Wording (Variants):

How would you decide which work to do first?

Why They Ask This Question

The interviewer wants to know if you're responsible enough to do your work on your own or whether someone has to keep reminding you. This is a very important concern for most hiring managers. If they have to keep telling you, then you become a potential liability – a bad hire right off the bat. Thus, you want to assure them you're a self-starter who can prioritize.

Ideal Answer

Prioritizing and planning my work is always an integral part of my working style. I always make sure to start my work as early as possible so that I'll have a lot of buffer. I also prefer to finish everything within time and would hate to have work left over.

To keep track of my work, I always maintain a to-do list. I prioritize tasks based on importance and urgency. Most important and urgent tasks take first priority, important but not urgent ones next, urgent but not important ones third and neither of these last. I also consider the effort required for each task, whether one task is dependent on another and things like that. I clearly communicate with my team members to make sure we align on priorities and adjust as needed.

I often revisit my to-do list and update the changes. Online tools make this easier. My plans and to-do lists are comprehensive yet flexible so that any future changes or shifting of priorities can be accommodated.

Never Say

Don't blank out on this question. Don't think the question is redundant. Don't give one-line answers like "It depends on the situation" or "Priority is based on importance" and stop with that. Many points from the above ideal answer might seem obvious, but are still necessary to assure the interviewer. It creates some trust in you as a good prioritizer.

How to Say It

Be enthusiastic to answer this question. This is an excellent opportunity to show your value. Explain that your prioritizing process is both strong and adaptable at the same time. Keep it short and clear. You may even want to tailor the given answer to your line of work.

Why This Answer Works

The given answer covers all the points that most interviewers will want to hear in this situation. This answer is suitable for almost every role or field. It clearly assures the interviewer that you have a solid approach toward keeping priorities and it won't be a problem for you.

Question 44

What do you look for when you hire people?

Alternative Wording (Variants):

What is your hiring style?

Why They Ask This Question

They typically ask this question for a manager or HR role. They want to know your hiring approach because this is a crucial part of your job. The best answer you can give is to say you'll hire based on requirements, company policy and the candidate's fit for the role. If they ask further questions, you can say you'll ask personality-type and behavioral-type questions to understand more about them.

Ideal Answer

I understand that hiring employees is going to be one of my very important responsibilities. When it comes to this, I'll first go through the job requirements and understand them correctly. Then, I'll shortlist resumes based on the requirements, qualifications, experience, skill set and other relevant attributes. Once we get to the interview stage, I'll ask the right set of questions that will test both the technical capabilities as well as the behavioral or attitude-related traits of the candidate. From my end, I'll check if the candidate shows seriousness, understanding, commitment, professionalism, diligence, clear communication, stress tolerance, tactfulness, and their fit with the company. While doing all this, I'll also be mindful of the company's hiring policies and practices. I'll make sure to consult with my team members and HR before making a final decision.

Never Say

Never say you don't have a hiring style. Never say you'll hire based on requirements and stop with that. Don't get turned off by this question or show disinterest. Don't give one-word or two-word answers. Doing any of these will make you look bad. Instead, describe the steps you'll take even if they seem obvious to you.

How to Say It

Answer this question with full enthusiasm. Make sure your answer is comprehensive to include requirements, qualifications, experience, personality, soft skills and fit with this company. Yet, keep it short and to the point. Say you'll also take into account company policies and practices. This is mandatory. Make sure you include a word about consulting with your team members, while still conveying that you're bold enough to make the decision. This will show that you are both collaborative and courageous. Keep your answer as general as possible so that it can fit with most interviewers' expectations.

Why This Answer Works

This given answer works because it covers everything an interviewer would want to hear. While different interviewers have different expectations, the given answer stays generic enough to suit all situations.

201

Question 45

How would you decide which task to delegate to whom?

Alternative Wording (Variants):

What is your task delegation style?

Why They Ask This Question

This question is comparable to the previous one. Delegating tasks depends on several factors like the work at hand, its importance, its urgency, costs involved and people available. It is difficult to answer this question without context. So, it's best to give a generic answer suitable for all situations.

Ideal Answer

I understand that delegating tasks is a very important activity in this role. When I delegate, I want to maximize work quality and efficiency. I want the work to be done quickly and affordably without compromising quality.

For this, I'll first evaluate the work to be done in terms of its importance, urgency, cost, time and difficulty. Side by side, I'll also consider each team member's experience level, skill set, and workload capacity. This will help me decide the best suited person for each task.

Communication is key to effective delegation. So, I'll clearly instruct each team member on their tasks and maintain open lines of communication. I'll monitor the progress and support everyone as needed. Once completed, I'll give everyone credit and constructive feedback, reinforcing their strengths and pointing out areas for improvement.

Never Say

Never say you don't have a delegation style or you don't know your style. Don't give an uninspiring one-line answer.

How to Say It

Keep it short and to the point. Show full enthusiasm. Show that you'll have the best interests of the company at heart and be tactful with your team members. Tell them you'll communicate smoothly and give feedback for improvement.

Why This Answer Works

This answer works because it fits all delegation situations and will be convincing to most interviewers.

Question 46

How do you usually decide whom to promote?

Alternative Wording (Variants):

What do you look for in an employee when evaluating their suitability for a promotion?

Why They Ask This Question

This question is fairly straightforward. They want to know what factors you'll consider when promoting. While a lot of it depends on the specifics of each case, you can give them a general idea.

Ideal Answer

Whom to promote is a crucial decision. I understand that it can be tough, and as a manager, I might have to do this a lot. While the candidates' performance and experience are basic things to check, other qualities such as attitude, leadership potential, and cooperativeness are also pivotal. I typically look at each candidate's track record, capacity to handle more responsibility, willingness to improve and tactfulness. I'll also seek feedback from supervisors, peers, and direct reports before deciding. Ultimately, I'll promote those who showed strong commitment, leadership potential, and positive impact.

Never Say

Don't say "It depends" or "There are a lot of factors" etc. and stop with that. Don't give one-line answers as it will sound dismissive and diffident. Don't feel lost by the genericness of this question. Don't talk about a specific promotion decision you made, unless they ask you for one specifically. As long as the question is general, keep the answer generic.

How to Say It

Show full interest when answering this question. Give an overall rundown of all the factors that go into a promotion decision. At the same time, keep it short and to the point.

Why This Answer Works

This answer works because it lists all the usual factors that a manager would normally consider while making a promotion decision. This answer would fit most interviewers' expectations.

Question 47

Have you ever had to fire people? What were the reasons, and how did you handle the situation?

Alternative Wording (Variants):

Tell me about a time when you had to lay off someone.
If you had to let an employee go, how would you execute it?

Why They Ask This Question

Terminating or laying off an employee who has worked with you on a daily basis is never easy. It's an unpleasant but also a necessary part of work life. As a manager, you're expected to carry out the termination process as often as the company wants you to. You shouldn't feel hesitant to do it.

Example Answer

In my previous role as the manager at a retail store, I had to make the difficult decision to fire an employee for consistently underperforming and not meeting the expectations.

Before taking any action, I documented every instance where the employee had not met expectations and had been given opportunities to improve. I also held a meeting with HR and my bosses to ensure that all necessary protocols and procedures were followed.

When it was time to inform that employee, I called them into a private room and made sure no one could hear us. I started by acknowledging the employee's efforts and discussing the areas where they were struggling. I politely informed them that they were being terminated and clarified the reasons for doing so. I provided specific examples to show their performance wasn't meeting the company standard. I showed enough empathy and professionalism. I didn't want them to take this the wrong way.

I also listened to what they had to say and offered support in their transition, such as helping with job search and providing a positive reference. While the employee was certainly not happy, they understood the situation and accepted my decision. It was definitely a tough conversation, but I knew it was necessary for the team's overall success.

Never Say

Never say you hesitated to do it. Likewise, don't say you did it in a very blunt and rude tone either. Both of these will make you seem unfit for firing people. Tell them you showed empathy but never hesitation.

How to Say It

Keep the incident simple. Mention the relevant facts. Highlight that it was difficult for you, but you never backed off or hesitated from doing it.

Why Such an Answer Works

This answer works because it covers everything the interviewer wants to hear. The fact that this is a difficult task but you still followed all protocols, smoothly discussed with the employee, gave them enough chances while still being polite and professional is precisely what interviewers expect.

Question 48

How long would it take for you to start making a meaningful contribution to our firm?

Alternative Wording (Variants):

How long do you expect your training to last?

Why They Ask This Question

This may sound like an unfair question. Maybe it is. The interviewer asks how long it'll take you to fully acquaint yourself with the job and start working to your fullest. This is impossible to answer as you have no idea about the job's difficulty, work environment and expectations. So, all you can do is assure them that you'll take the least amount of time and start contributing quickly. Don't give out an actual duration as you have no idea.

Ideal Answer

I want to tell you that I am very excited to begin this job. I feel very positive about joining here because I heard a lot of good things about this company. I heard that you provide quality training and ample guidance to new employees. I want to assure you that I am a fast learner. I always do a lot of homework during my training phase so that I learn everything as soon as possible. I am sure with your quality training and my enthusiasm we can hit the ground running in no time.

Never Say

Don't feel discouraged by this question. Don't show any discomfort. Don't say you don't know or it depends etc. Most importantly, don't give them an actual time frame as you have no idea. If you did, your manager might hold you to it later on. Just use words like "as soon as possible", "as quickly as practical", "in no time" etc. to answer it.

How to Say It

Be very excited and positive as you say it. This is an opportunity to show how fast a learner you are. Show enthusiasm to learn and perform quickly. Relieve the interviewer of any worries and build trust in you.

Why This Answer Works

This answer works because it shows confidence and positivity. It clearly states that you're willing to learn and contribute quickly but doesn't mention an actual time period. This should emotionally assure the interviewer while logically leaving your options open. This is the best way to answer this question without getting into an unintended commitment.

Question 49

What do you know about this industry?

Alternative Wording (Variants):

What important trends do you see in our industry?
What are the pressing issues in our industry?
Can you share your knowledge about this industry?

Why They Ask This Question

The interviewer wants to make sure you have well-rounded knowledge about the industry. They are trying to understand if you know anything at all about the industry and if your particular experience (the projects you dealt with) matches with their requirements (the projects and goals they have). It's very difficult to give a single ideal answer here. You have to come up with your own answer that's specific to your industry and work experience. The examples given below might help.

Example Answer 1

I have been working as a nurse for five years. If my prior experience has taught me anything, it's that healthcare is a constantly evolving industry. Technology and medical research have advanced a lot. Healthcare providers must stay up to date with best practices and guidelines to provide effective treatments. Compliance with laws and regulations has become even more important these days. It's a highly regulated industry with strict protocols for patient safety and quality care. In recent years, the industry has been facing challenges such as rising costs, increasing demand, staff shortage, insurance problems, and tough competition. Thus, hospital employees, especially nurses like me, must put in extra time and care into work to ensure patient satisfaction. This is crucial in keeping up a good reputation for the hospital and to stand out in competition. Overall, working in this industry is both interesting and challenging, as it allows you to provide essential medical care to individuals and communities.

Example Answer 2

I have been a car salesman for 20 years. One trend I see in recent times is the demand for electric cars. Consumers are becoming more aware of how their actions affect the environment. They think of electric cars as an eco-friendly substitute. There's also a general opinion that electric cars are low on maintenance. Plus, given the recent price drop, more and more customers want to buy electric cars. At the same time, since this is a fairly new product, there are so many things we can't be sure of yet. For instance, the profit margins of electric cars have gone down due to competition, the product is not yet standardized and charging stations are still not commonplace. The sustainability of after-sales service also remains to be seen. Even so, despite these risk factors, there has been a steady rise in the overall demand for electric cars. All in all, electric cars can be profitable provided we carefully strategize sales and educate customers amply.

Example Answer 3

My experience in the web development industry spans four decades. I began my career in the '90s when websites were virtually just colorful text documents with hyperlinks. Then, slightly more complex sites came up with morphing images, flashing text and videos. The 2000s saw the rise of dynamic websites, which could interact with users and update in real time. This was when Adobe Flash-based sites became popular. Every business started creating their online presence. Websites began specializing in what they do such as entertainment, information, promotion or sales. Social media websites became a thing around this time, redefining user experience. Then, the 2010s came – this time period saw the rise of HTML5, CSS3 and the phasing out of Adobe Flash, which was a huge technical leap. The advent of smartphones and tablets revolutionized the way we access the internet. Websites started becoming more responsive to accommodate tablet and mobile users. Websites also upped their game in terms of security, professional design and increased functionality. Today, we live in the 2020s where the web has become an inseparable part of our lives. It sits in everybody's pocket. In recent years, one trend I notice is the use of AI in almost every website. Whether it's for a chatbot, SEO, design, code generation or even image enhancement, AI is here to stay. While AI has both risks and benefits, its efficiency makes it worth using. While all this is great, one challenge I notice today is security. Data breaches and data vandalism have become commonplace. Even big tech companies have this problem. Thus, many website owners are putting mammoth effort into security. Overall, I feel the industry is taking an interesting turn right now. Internet has penetrated everywhere, even underdeveloped countries. It excites me to wait and see what new surprises are in store for us as technology progresses.

Never Say

Don't be dumbfounded by this question. Don't say you have no idea about the trends and issues. Don't talk about something unrelated, and definitely, don't make negative-sounding comments about the industry.

How to Say It

The interviewer wants to know if you have analyzed the industry and understood the current situation. So, be specific about the trends and issues you pick out. Give examples where necessary. It doesn't matter what you choose to talk about as long as it's true, positive and relevant. Ideally, pick one trend and one challenge, and mention one or two sentences about each. If you can't be specific, it's also okay to give a short rundown of how the industry operates in general.

Why Such Answers Work

Essentially, the interviewer wants you to demonstrate a strong understanding about the industry. This understanding becomes the basis on which you perform your daily work. Any answer that takes inspiration from the given answers will work for this purpose.

Question 50

What should I know that's not on your resume?

Alternative Wording (Variants):

Tell me something that you haven't included on your resume.

Is there anything else that I should know about you?

Do you want to tell me anything else about you that we have not discussed so far?

Why They Ask This Question

Even if you're a highly experienced interviewee, this question could catch you off guard if you're not prepared. While you can always say something on the spot, it'll never be as good as giving a well-prepared answer. So, it's best to think of an answer beforehand but say it like you only thought of it on the spot. It's also best if you use this answer to highlight some other good quality you have. You can take the following example answers as an inspiration to come up with your own.

Example Answer 1 (Improving Yourself Career Wise)

In my free time, I attend private classes related to my field, so that I can continually improve myself and stay up to date. This not only helps me improve but also meet other professionals in my field. From them, I often hear about new experiences and innovations. It's also a good networking platform to share ideas and team up on projects. I can honestly tell you that these classes have helped me get better at my work.

Example Answer 2 (Volunteering)

One thing that's not on my resume is my passion for volunteer work. I have been actively involved in community service for the past five years. I work with local shelters, food drive organizers, and fundraising events for various causes. Giving back to the community is extremely important to me. I believe that it's essential to use our skills and resources to help those in need. This experience has shaped me into a more empathetic person, and I always find new ways to make a positive impact in the world.

Example Answer 3 (Hobby)

In my free time, I like to do gardening. I own a small piece of land next to my house where I grow a handful of flowers, fruits and vegetables. I make sure to water them daily and do the right maintenance. Once ready, I collect the flowers and produce. My family and I take what we need and give out the rest of the produce to neighbors and friends. I started small but now my garden has become sizable. This is something that relaxes me and I am quite proud of doing it.

Never Say

Don't say you have included everything in your resume. Don't say there's nothing else you can think of. While this question is not a deal-breaker as such, not being prepared for this may not end the interview on a smooth note.

How to Say It

Pick one thing to say. Make sure it's something that will definitely make a good impression about you. Mention one or two details about what you do, how you do it and how it has helped you. Keep it short and simple.

Why Such Answers Work

Any answer you come up with based on the given answers is going to work. Such answers use this question as one more opportunity to share something positive about you. The idea is to increase your reputation. Interviewers usually ask this question just to end things on a sweet note. That's precisely what the given answers do.

Question 51

When can you start?

Alternative Wording (Variants):

When can you join?
What is the notice period policy at your current job?
When is the earliest you can start working for us?

Why They Ask This Question

This is one of the easiest questions to answer. Once offered the job, employers expect you to join at the earliest. So, the answer is either right away if you're unemployed, or at the end of your notice period if you're employed. If you really want this job, you should be eager to start ASAP.

Some employers will give you time (mostly a few days) to think about this offer. Others will want an immediate answer. It all depends on their urgency.

From your end, if you want this job, it's best to say so then and there. If you really need time to think, it's okay to say that too, but remember that you're taking a risk – some employers won't wait for your response even if they promised to. They may go with the next available candidate. Whatever the case, don't keep them waiting too long. Most employers will appreciate a response within two business days.

Ideal Answer (Assuming You Want This Job)

Oh, I am happy that you're offering me this job. I can join as soon I finish my current job's notice period, which I believe is two weeks. I'll confirm this to you in two business days after a discussion with my current boss. If everything goes well, I'll finish all the relieving procedures and join here within the said time. I'll keep you posted in the meantime. I am enthusiastically looking forward to working here.

Never Say

If you want the job, don't ask for time to think. Given the competition these days, someone else will fill your place within that time. In case you give them false hope that you will join, but later went back on your word, don't expect them to do you any favors later on (especially if you change your mind).

How to Say It

Show thankfulness that they are offering you this job. Whether you can join immediately or need to serve notice period, be frank about it. If your notice period or relieving procedure is taking longer than expected, keep them updated. Be honest with the reasons too. At all times, be available over phone call and e-mail. Your candidness and availability will be seen as a huge positive.

Why This Answer Works

This answer works because it begins with showing happiness for the job offer and then goes on to frankly say when you can join, followed by what you'll do in the meantime and ending with the eagerness to start working. This neatly sums up frankness and professionalism in one short and sweet reply.

Question 52

Sell me this pen.

Alternative Wording (Variants):

Sell me [insert name of article here].

Why They Ask This Question

They'll most likely ask this question if your job involves sales. They want to know if you understand personal selling, the steps in it and your people skills. Selling is a very special skill in any business that can be improved with training and practice.

This question is crucial as it directly tests your skill level. You want to nail this one. Don't let this challenge intimidate you. Accept it with enthusiasm. Also, while you're geared up to do this, realize that there is no guarantee that you'll succeed. You're after all selling the interviewer's own pen back to them. Your success depends on how lenient the interviewer is honestly. However, don't let this deter you. Give it your best shot.

To do this correctly, you want to understand the process of selling in three steps.

Sales Process

Step #1: Understanding Needs (Empathizing)

You first want to keep the pen down (or put it in your coat pocket) and start asking questions about their need for a pen. Ask questions like "Do you use a pen?", "How often do you use a pen?", "What do you use it for?" etc. As a rule of thumb for pen in particular, the higher someone's position is, the less they'll use a pen. People in high positions tend to use pens sparingly – only for signing documents and such. People of lower positions however may use a pen extensively – write entire letters, documents, reports and so on. Secretaries use a pen for taking notes.

Get your interviewer to talk at length about their need for a pen. Be patient and keep trying until you can get them talking. After that, actively listen to them. You can get a lot of useful information that can help you make the sale.

The interviewer may answer your questions honestly. If they do, your job is much easier. Sometimes, the interviewer may also reply curtly and dismissively. If this happens, realize they're testing you harshly. Don't let this deter you, and don't take it personally. Keep going.

Ask questions to which the interviewer is likely to answer "Yes". For instance, "Since you're the director of this company, you'll use pens a lot for signing documents, won't you?" or "Using a pen that's considered high status will increase your image as the president of this company, right?". The quicker you get them to say yes and the more often you get them to say yes, the more likely they'll accept your sale.

Overall, in this first step, you want to make your prospect (interviewer in this case) feel understood. They have to open up to you. Ideally, they must talk about their needs and problems. Once you feel you have done all this, you can move to the next step.

Step #2: Identifying an Opening (A Specific Problem, Opportunity or Need)

This is a very important step. In fact the whole purpose of the previous step is to get to this. You want to identify a very specific problem, an area to improve or a need the customer has. This is called an opening. Some customers may be aware of this opening. Some others may not have even realized or noticed it yet. You could be the first to notice and tell them. Either way, check if they show interest in solving that problem or satisfying that need. If they show interest, you have almost made the sale! This is the core part of this process.

When talking about the problem, make sure you talk about it in such an alluring way that they feel you have perfectly understood their problem. Human beings always have the need to be understood and empathized with. You need to describe to them very specific details about their problem and the emotions they go through so that they warm up to you.

For selling the pen, you can say something like "Tell me whether this happens to you. During important meetings, some clients may judge you harshly before signing a high-value contract crucial to your business. Everything from the car you drive, the suit you wear and how well you speak is seen with a critical eye. You must feel uneasy when they give you that brutal, judgmental look and you have no idea what they think about you. You're worried whether they'll sign the contract or not." Most high-position interviewers would've gone through something like this. Mostly, they'll agree with you. Very few interviewers deliberately choose to be all bottled up. So, be confident as you talk about their problem in detail.

Before going to Step #3, you must have empathized enough (Step #1) and spoken about their problems such that they feel understood (Step #2). At this point, your potential buyer should be relaxed and open. Human beings agree to emotion, not logic.

Step #3: The Pitch (The Solution, Closing the Sale)

This is what you have built up to so far. Here's where you want to present your product (or service) as the solution to their problem. If you have done the previous steps correctly, the listener would be most receptive by now. You can describe how good your product is and what it can do for them.

When you present your product as the solution, be direct but not too direct that it sounds rude or desperate. Be specific about how the product will solve their problem. Use more emotional words and phrases that continue showing empathy and understanding. Create a very realistic picture in their mind of your product directly solving their problem. Make sure the prospect feels ecstatic that their problem is going away. Make it so enticing that they are impatient to buy your product on the spot.

To sell the pen to the interviewer, here is what you can say: "When it comes to tough situations like these (judgmental client meetings), you don't want your client to judge you based on something small like a pen. Luckily, I got you covered. (Take the pen out of your coat pocket) This pen is an expensive, luxury pen from a highly respected brand, regarded as one of *the* best all over the world. Famous presidents, CEOs and directors of some of the *Fortune* 500 companies are known to use this pen. Celebrities, sportspersons and heads of state are known to use it for autographs, contracts and such. This pen comes with a golden nib, ergonomic handle and a thick exterior. It's strong enough to resist high amounts of pressure just like the people that use it. It comes in a beautiful case. Oh, did I tell you it has a lifetime service warranty? That's right – lifetime. You bring it to us for repair anytime and we'll fix it up like new for you. Overall, by using this pen, you can create a rock-solid good impression on your client. Your client will always think high of you, no doubt. They'll be willing to sign many more expensive contracts with you. When you buy this pen, you're not just buying a pen, you're buying your clients' trust in you. You're buying your entry ticket to high-value contracts. So, you want your high-value contracts? Buy this pen."

Majority of interviewers will accept the above pitch. Even if they didn't say yes verbally, they may appreciate your innovative approach and vivid descriptions. While most interviewers will accept, realize that there will always be some interviewers who are hard to satisfy.

Since this is only a pretense situation and the interviewer has no real need for a pen, they can always say no. If not, they may inquire about the price of the pen and then say no. If any of these two happen, present the pen as a free sample for the interviewer to use. Since this is a free sample, there's no harm in taking it. This way, you can logically justify your pitch later on. One way or the other, you have convinced them to take it – you made the sale! This is a great way to handle the situation given the kind of challenge they are throwing at you.

You might think the pitch above is exaggerated and it takes a lot of liberties. Contrary to what you might think, this is what goes into making a sales pitch. Remember how we talked about TV commercials earlier in this book? This is also where it applies. For most situations (even real sales situations), this pitch will work if you have already made them feel relaxed and brought them to an emotional state where they are open to agreeing with you.

If the customer is emotionally ready to accept your proposal, they'll not ask many questions.

Since this is a mock sale, your interviewer might either agree with you or press you for more questions. If they ask you questions like "How do you know so much about this pen?", you can always say "Since this is just a mock exercise, I came up with the details. In a real sale, I'll educate myself enough about the product well before engaging with a customer".

In summary, this is the classic three-step sales process useful for any sales situation. Most interviewers will be okay with this approach. In a fair interview, you'll score a lot of points if you follow this process.

A Word of Caution

Some interviewers might use this as a stress interview (abusive interview) question. They will use it as a way to insult you into leaving the room. They usually do this to eliminate as many candidates as possible. They may ask too many testing questions, be unimpressed or uninterested in your sales efforts or even mock you for making an attempt. You want to identify this early on, even if the signs are mild. If this happens, evaluate if it's worth continuing the interview. Such an employer isn't worth working for. Leave quickly. Don't take it personally or feel hurt. Understand they are just doing their job of eliminating candidates. Post it somewhere online so that future candidates can know.

Never Say

Never directly talk about the pen. Don't start with the features of the pen or what the pen will do for them. Always start with the needs of the buyer and then work toward your product. Make sure everything you say is relevant. Don't feel nervous or diffident at any point in this process. If they decide to test you with too many questions, don't be frustrated or alarmed.

Don't act too smart. Don't act cocky like they show in movies. This is not your time to play the hero – this is the time to be humble and accept the challenge that this is.

There's a lot of bad advice everywhere for this question. Like some bad advice involves you walking out with the pen as a power move. Don't walk out with the pen thinking that the interviewer will ask it back from you and then you can negotiate. If you do this, the interviewer might either let you walk away with the pen (a pen may not mean much for them) or, if they negotiate, they won't like you for putting them in that situation. Thus, even if you technically succeeded with the sale, they won't hire you. They risk losing a pen but you risk losing a job!

How to Say It

Show a lot of finesse in handling this process. Show ample professionalism. Be patient until you identify an opening

(Step #2). It can take a while. Be smooth, positive and confident when making your pitch. Say it in a way that the interviewer gets a new perspective on their own pen. Don't rush through anything. In case you can't make the sale, accept it. The interviewer will most likely understand.

Why This Approach Works

This approach works because it follows a time-tested three-step principle to make a sale. This method clearly demonstrates that you're a good salesperson and you have understood the sales process. This is much more important than whether you actually made the sale. This approach exhibits several good qualities such as patience, good communication, positivity, people skills, confidence, emotional intelligence and adaptability.

Question 53

Do you have any questions for us?

Alternative Wording (Variants):

Is there anything you want to ask us?

Why They Ask This Question

This is a very important question. You definitely want to show that you have questions for them and make sure the questions are the right kind. Your questions should show that you have carefully considered this job and are committed to the organization's business. This is a fantastic opportunity to make a lasting impression before leaving the interview.

If they don't give you a chance to ask your questions, seek permission to do so. However, if they seem uninterested in your questions, realize that you're dealing with a one-sided employer, i.e., a bad employer. Evaluate if you really want to work for someone like this. On the contrary, if they show interest in answering your questions, that's a sign they may be a good employer.

When it comes to what you can ask, there's no single definitive list of questions that will suit every situation, but the following list should help.

Good Questions to Ask the Interviewer

- What is the next stage of the selection process?
- When can I get back to you after today?

- Can you give me an overview of this company's culture?
- How has the company progressed over recent years?
- Which team will I be placed in and what is it like working there?
- What does a typical work day look like in my role?
- How can I prepare myself to give the best performance here?
- Which client or clients will I be working for? What should I know about them?
- What are the biggest challenges facing the team, department or organization right now?
- Can you share more about the onboarding process for new employees?
- What do you love most about working here?

Ask only 2-3 of these questions and not more. Note that the sole purpose of such questions is to show your eagerness to get started. Some of these questions are also meant for the interviewer to imagine you in the role, doing your everyday tasks. If you can get them to imagine you in the role, it dramatically increases your chance of getting hired.

Terrible Questions to Ask the Interviewer

- I have no questions. I have no idea what to ask. (Shows lack of interest.)
- Did I get the job? (You'll be notified later. You should give them time.)

- Any questions about salary, overtime, perks etc. (Not something to be asked at the end of the interview but during the interview might be okay depending on a lot of things.)
- Any questions about leave policy, weekends and holidays. (Shows that you're more interested in leaves than working.)
- Any questions about how long you're supposed to stay at work each day, whether work hours are flexible, whether you can come in late and leave early. (Shows that you're only interested in coming in late or leaving early.)
- Any questions about promotions and pay raise. (Employers don't want candidates who seek promotions and pay raises.)
- Any questions that suggest you'll do other useless tasks during work hours. For instance, don't ask if social media sites are accessible from office computers.
- Any questions that might imply you have regular commitments outside of work and want to frequently attend them. (This means you'll often come late, leave early or take more leaves to attend those commitments.)
- Any questions with the slightest hint of wanting to work remotely, unless otherwise they specified this already. (Companies hate employees who want to work remotely.)

- Any question that shows desperation for the job. (There is a fine line between being enthusiastic and being desperate.)
- Any question that focuses too far into the future. (Interviewers are more concerned about your immediate joining and performance rather than some distant possibility.)

Chapter 6
Working the Interview Magic

Job hunt is an artificial situation. While it may look simple on the outset, understanding employers' expectations and implied meanings is one tough nut to crack. Don't worry though.

Every topic discussed in this book will ease this problem by a million times. You can easily apply what you've learned from all the previous chapters, by simply remembering the most crucial points. These points are summarized below.

Important Points to Remember

#1 – Merit Makes You Qualified, but Soft Skills Get You Hired

This must be obvious by now, but still easy to forget in a moment of hurry. A typical employer may compromise on lack of skill, but they'll never overlook the times you were rude, selfish, indifferent, unprofessional, inflexible or uncooperative.

#2 – You Got Only One Shot at This

As brutal as it may seem, there are no second chances in interviews. First impression is the only impression. You approach it wrong the first time, you've already given them a reason to reject you.

#3 – Employers Are Myopic

Employers have a very narrow window to see you through and draw conclusions about you. Based on this, they decide whether or not to hire you. It's your job to show your best side within that window. This includes answering their questions with only those answers that they want to hear.

#4 – What They Say They Want and What They Really Want Are Different

This is a tricky one even for those well experienced in giving interviews. Many times, it's hard to find out what a hirer really wants. They often say something but mean something else. While you can take their words as an initial basis, don't take them for granted. Read between the lines.

#5 – The Process Is Never Transparent; You'll Never Know What They Really Think of You

Unless the interviewer lets you know, you can never know whether you're answering the questions right or wrong. They may act unimpressed while actually being impressed or vice versa. It's not under your control. So, don't fret over interviews while still giving your best.

#6 – You'll Always Get Questions You Didn't Prepare for

The previous Q&A chapter is meant as a guide on how to approach interview questions. There is no fixed list of questions anybody can give you that'll include every single possibility. Having said this, you can take cues from the given answers in order to answer other questions that you may find difficult. As a rule, you should always expect tough questions at interviews that make you feel dumbstruck. It's easier to deal with them when you expect them.

#7 – Every Interview Is an Energy-Draining and Confidence-Draining Experience

This is all the more true if the job you're applying for is competitive. They want to test every candidate to the limit to find out the best one. If an interview feels exhausting, that's because it's meant to be. Once you understand this, interviews start becoming a lot more manageable.

#8 – The Job Requirements Is Just a Wish List

A hirer with unrealistic expectations in the job ad is likely to compromise on them during the interview. The scary wording might just be a trick to make applicants self-select themselves out of the interview. Don't let the job posting deter you from applying.

#9 – Get Them to Imagine You in the Role ASAP

The sooner you can make them imagine you in the role and the more frequently you can get them to imagine you in the role, the higher your chances are for getting hired. This is because, psychologically, we tend to readily do those things that we can form a mental picture of. To get them to imagine you in the role, talk more about how you'll perform the day-to-day activities, the practical situations you'll face and the improvements you'll bring to the table. Ask questions such that the interviewer will clearly imagine you in the role.

#10 – Trap Questions Are Tough and For Good Reason

There were several trap questions mentioned as such in the Q&A chapter. The trap questions make it look like you'll fail either way. They're deliberately meant to be so. If you choose any one side of a trap question and are hasty about answering it, you're more likely to fail. The trick is to be patient and think of a neutral answer. Answering trap questions without falling into the trap can score more points than other questions. If anything, you should see trap questions as a way to score more.

#11 – Big Name Is Big Game

A candidate who has been part of highly regarded organizations may be valued as "better", even if their actual skills are subpar. This is another easy way for hirers to justify hiring decisions to their bosses.

#12 – Desperation for the Job Is the Quickest Way to Shoot Yourself in the Foot

Hirers often see desperate candidates as a better option because they think such candidates will accept a lower salary. However, the moment they see an actual desperate candidate, they're immediately put off by them. This is an ironic situation! Being desperate only makes you look bad in the eyes of the potential employer. Desperation also means you'll be compromising on a lot of benefits and end up losing any edge. You want to be humble and nice but never desperate for a job.

#13 – Evaluate the Organization and the People for Yourself

The job interview is a chance for you to evaluate if you want to work for that organization. Based on how everyone at the company treats you and how the interview process is conducted, you can get a glimpse of the company's culture. In addition, you can also read employer reviews online. You should decide for yourself if you fit in there the same way they check your fit.

#14 – Social Media Plays a Key Role

Most employers check your social media profiles. This is a very accessible way for them to know more about your activities and you as a person. Make sure your professional social media profiles are up to date. Your personal profiles should be free from controversy and vulgarity.

#15 – Follow Up Even if You're Not Very Confident

Send a follow-up e-mail or make a follow-up phone call just once to check if they have selected you. This is a great way to let them know that you're truly interested in the job. Chances are they either forgot about you or didn't think you'll be interested. Following up should fix both of these. Don't call or send e-mail more than once as it might make you seem desperate.

Chapter 7
Your Path to Interview Success

Interviewing is a skill. And any skill can be mastered with practice. While a job interview is a moderately serious affair, it's nothing to be anxious about. Always think of job interviews as opportunities for growth and advancement. Your dream job is just around the corner, and job interview is the door that leads to it. So, keep searching and applying for jobs, because your golden opportunity is out there somewhere waiting for you. Embrace every interview as a chance to showcase your skills and potential. Stay resilient, stay focused, and stay optimistic, because the job market is what you make of it.

THANK YOU FOR READING!